FIRST DAY DEVOTIONS

Inspirational, Encouraging and Uplifting
Weekly Devotionals

BY DONNA JUNKER

GREEN WINE™
FAMILY BOOKS

FIRST DAY DEVOTIONS

Inspirational, Encouraging and Uplifting Weekly Devotionals

Copyright © 2017 by Donna Kasik Junker

Library of Congress Control Number: 2016958399

Junker, Donna Kasik, 1961—

ISBN 978-1-935434-87-0

Subject Codes and Description: 1. REL: 045000: Religion: Christian Ministry – Missions; 2. REL: 116000: Religion: Intolerance, Persecution & Conflict; 3. REL: 063000: Religion: Christian Life – Stewardship and Giving.

The writer acknowledges the editorial assistance of Joshua Collins and GEA Press. All rights reserved, including the right to reproduce this book or any part thereof in any form, except for inclusion of brief quotations in a review, without the written permission of the author and GlobalEdAdvancePRESS.

Printed in Australia, Brazil, France, Germany, Italy, Spain, Poland, UK, and USA.

Also, available on Espresso Book Machine© or any place good books are sold.

Book Cover Design by Global Graphics (NYC).

The Press does not have ownership of the contents of a book; this is the author's work and the author owns the copyright. All theories, concepts, theological constructs, and ecclesiastical perspectives are those of the author and not necessarily the Press. They are presented for open and free discussion of the issues involved. All comments and feedback should be directed to the Email: [comments4author@aol.com] and the comments will be forwarded to the author for response.

Published by

GreenWine Family Books[tm]

a division of GlobalEdAdvance Press

All Old Testament verses are taken from *The New Oxford Annotated Bible New Revised Version*, Edited by Bruce M. Metzger and Roland E. Murphy, New York: Oxford University Press, 1994.

All New Testament verses are taken from *The EVERGREEN Devotional New Testament* (EDNT) - Community and Family Education Edition (C.A.F.E.), By Hollis L. Green, Nashville. Post-Gutenberg Books, GlobalEdAdvancePRESS. 2015, unless noted.

DEDICATION

This book is dedicated to my husband,

Dr. Paul Junker

The love and inspiration of my life,

And with whom I share devotions each morning.

~

L. O. V. E. is:

L- learning from the past.

O- opening your heart to someone.

V- viewing the future with confidence.

E- enjoying the present moment.

2017 Calendar

January 2017

Su	Mo	Tu	We	Th	Fr	Sa
1	2	3	4	5	6	7
8	9	10	11	12	13	14
15	16	17	18	19	20	21
22	23	24	25	26	27	28
29	30	31				

February 2017

Su	Mo	Tu	We	Th	Fr	Sa
			1	2	3	4
5	6	7	8	9	10	11
12	13	14	15	16	17	18
19	20	21	22	23	24	25
26	27	28				

March 2017

Su	Mo	Tu	We	Th	Fr	Sa
			1	2	3	4
5	6	7	8	9	10	11
12	13	14	15	16	17	18
19	20	21	22	23	24	25
26	27	28	29	30	31	

April 2017

Su	Mo	Tu	We	Th	Fr	Sa
						1
2	3	4	5	6	7	8
9	10	11	12	13	14	15
16	17	18	19	20	21	22
23	24	25	26	27	28	29
30						

May 2017

Su	Mo	Tu	We	Th	Fr	Sa
	1	2	3	4	5	6
7	8	9	10	11	12	13
14	15	16	17	18	19	20
21	22	23	24	25	26	27
28	29	30	31			

June 2017

Su	Mo	Tu	We	Th	Fr	Sa
				1	2	3
4	5	6	7	8	9	10
11	12	13	14	15	16	17
18	19	20	21	22	23	24
25	26	27	28	29	30	

July 2017

Su	Mo	Tu	We	Th	Fr	Sa
						1
2	3	4	5	6	7	8
9	10	11	12	13	14	15
16	17	18	19	20	21	22
23	24	25	26	27	28	29
30	31					

August 2017

Su	Mo	Tu	We	Th	Fr	Sa
		1	2	3	4	5
6	7	8	9	10	11	12
13	14	15	16	17	18	19
20	21	22	23	24	25	26
27	28	29	30	31		

September 2017

Su	Mo	Tu	We	Th	Fr	Sa
					1	2
3	4	5	6	7	8	9
10	11	12	13	14	15	16
17	18	19	20	21	22	23
24	25	26	27	28	29	30

October 2017

Su	Mo	Tu	We	Th	Fr	Sa
1	2	3	4	5	6	7
8	9	10	11	12	13	14
15	16	17	18	19	20	21
22	23	24	25	26	27	28
29	30	31				

November 2017

Su	Mo	Tu	We	Th	Fr	Sa
			1	2	3	4
5	6	7	8	9	10	11
12	13	14	15	16	17	18
19	20	21	22	23	24	25
26	27	28	29	30		

December 2017

Su	Mo	Tu	We	Th	Fr	Sa
					1	2
3	4	5	6	7	8	9
10	11	12	13	14	15	16
17	18	19	20	21	22	23
24	25	26	27	28	29	30
31						

TABLE OF CONTENTS

FOREWORD
The Mission

In my work as a Chaplain/Pastoral Care Coordinator at the Lexington Rescue Mission in Lexington, Kentucky, part of my job is to write a weekly devotional for the staff. Each Wednesday afternoon I sit in my office, pray, and write my devotion, then email it to all of the staff. Each week several of the Mission staff sends me wonderfully kind and uplifting feedback from my devotions, which I do not deserve, but give glory to God if the devotionals have touched hearts and minds. After doing this part of my job for a couple of months, I decided to compile these devotions into a small book that could be used not only for the staff, but also for clients, and perhaps in homes and churches. I have included many of the devotions written at the Mission in this book and pray God uses them to uplift you as you begin your day.

I suggest reading the devotions in the morning, or whenever you set aside time each day to read your Bible. More importantly, focus on the Scripture readings throughout the day and week, keeping a journal of what you are learning as God uses His Word to transform your life. Try starting this book on a Sunday, read devotions on each Lord's Day, focusing on the words of Scripture, and keep a journal of your notes and reflections after each entry, which are provided for you in this book.

It is a privilege to work at the Lexington Rescue Mission. This Mission is a wonderful place that provides spiritual care and serves hot and nutritious meals to the poor and homeless in the community. Also provided are clothing, blankets, sleeping bags, toiletries, emergency utility and rent assistance, bus passes, transitional housing for those released from prison and/or recovering from addictions, job training, life skills, and re-entry programs for those coming out of prison. I am truly blessed to work at the Lexington Rescue Mission, and am grateful for the time given daily to read my Bible, pray, and write these devotions, along with my other roles as Pastoral Care Coordinator. If you are interested in the Lexington Rescue Mission, please go to their website at www.lexingtonrescue. org to learn about the Mission, their history, financials, staff, statement of faith, services, volunteer opportunities, events, how to donate and contact the Mission, and to follow their Blog.

Beginning to compile this little book, I thought of a short devotional story heard years ago. It is a parable called "The Ragman" about Jesus, who can take all of the old, dirty rags in our lives, and make them new. All of us, as the people each day at the Mission, are in need of giving our old dirty rags to Jesus in exchange for new clean cloths. It is a wonderful privilege to watch that transformation happen at the Mission, and I am personally thankful that my Lord and Savior replaced my dirty rags with fresh, clean clothing.

INTRODUCTORY STORY

"THE RAGMAN"

By Walter Wangerin, Jr.

I saw a strange sight. I stumbled upon a story most strange, like nothing my life, my street sense and my sly tongue had ever prepared me for. Hush, child. Hush, now, and I will tell it to you.

Even before the dawn one Friday morning I noticed a young man, handsome and strong, walking the alleys of our City. He was pulling an old cart filled with clothes both bright and new, and he was calling in a clear, tenor voice: "Rags!" Ah, the air was foul and the first light filthy to be crossed by such sweet music.

"Rags! New rags for old! I take your tired rags! Rags!"

"Now, this is a wonder," I thought to myself, for the man stood six-feet-four, and his arms were like tree limbs, hard and muscular, and his eyes flashed intelligence. Could he find no better job than this, to be a ragman in the inner city?

I followed him. My curiosity drove me. And I wasn't disappointed.

Soon the Ragman saw a woman sitting on her back porch. She was sobbing into a handkerchief, sighing, and shedding a thousand tears. Her knees and elbows made a sad X. Her shoulders shook. Her heart was breaking.

The Ragman stopped his cart. Quietly, he walked to the woman, stepping round tin cans, dead toys, and Pampers.

"Give me your rag," he said so gently, "and I'll give you another."

He slipped the handkerchief from her eyes. She looked up, and he laid across her palm a linen cloth so clean and new that it shined. She blinked from the gift to the giver.

Then, as he began to pull his cart again, the Ragman did a strange thing: he put her stained handkerchief to his own face; and then HE began to weep, to sob as grievously as she had done, his shoulders shaking. Yet she was left without a tear.

"This IS a wonder," I breathed to myself, and I followed the sobbing Ragman like a child who cannot turn away from mystery.

"Rags! Rags! New rags for old!"

In a little while, when the sky showed grey behind the rooftops and I could see the shredded curtains hanging out black windows, the Ragman came upon a girl whose head was wrapped in a bandage, whose eyes were empty. Blood soaked her bandage. A single line of blood ran down her cheek.

Now the tall Ragman looked upon this child with pity, and he drew a lovely yellow bonnet from his cart.

"Give me your rag," he said, tracing his own line on her cheek, "and I'll give you mine."

The child could only gaze at him while he loosened the bandage, removed it, and tied it to his own head. The bonnet he set on hers. And I gasped at what I saw: for with the bandage went the wound! Against his brow it ran a darker, more substantial blood – his own!

"Rags! Rags! I take old rags!" cried the sobbing, bleeding, strong, intelligent Ragman.

The sun hurt both the sky, now, and my eyes; the Ragman seemed more and more to hurry.

"Are you going to work?" he asked a man who leaned against a telephone pole. The man shook his head.

The Ragman pressed him: "Do you have a job?"

"Are you crazy?" sneered the other. He pulled away from the pole, revealing the right sleeve of his jacket – flat, the cuff stuffed into the pocket. He had no arm.

"So," said the Ragman. "Give me your jacket, and I'll give you mine."

Such quiet authority in his voice!

The one-armed man took off his jacket. So did the Ragman – and I trembled at what I saw: for the Ragman's arm stayed in its sleeve, and when the other put it on he had two good arms, thick as tree limbs; but the Ragman had only one.

"Go to work," he said.

After that he found a drunk, lying unconscious beneath an army blanket, and old man, hunched, wizened, and sick. He took that blanket and put it round himself, but for the drunk he left new clothes.

And now I had to run to keep up with the Ragman. Though he was weeping uncontrollably, and bleeding freely at the forehead, pulling his cart with one arm, stumbling for drunkenness, falling again and again, exhausted, old, old, and sick, yet he went with terrible speed. On spider's legs he skittered through the alleys of the City, this mile and the next, until he came to its limits, and then he rushed beyond.

I wept to see the change in this man. I hurt to see his sorrow. And yet I needed to see where he was going in such haste, perhaps to know what drove him so.

The little old Ragman – he came to a landfill. He came to the garbage pits. And then I wanted to help him in what he did, but I hung back, hiding. He climbed a hill. With tormented labor he cleared a little space on that hill. Then he sighed. He lay down. He pillowed his head on a handkerchief and a jacket. He covered his bones with an army blanket. And he died.

Oh, how I cried to witness that death! I slumped in a junked car and wailed and mourned as one who has no hope – because I had come to love the Ragman. Every other face had faded in the wonder of this man, and I cherished him; but he died. I sobbed myself to sleep.

I did not know – how could I know? – That I slept through Friday night and Saturday and its night, too.

But then, on Sunday morning, I was wakened by violence.

Light – pure, hard, demanding light – slammed against my sour face, and I blinked, and I looked, and I saw the last and the first wonder of all. There was the Ragman, folding the blanket most carefully, a scar on his forehead, but alive! And, besides that, healthy! There was no sign of sorrow nor of age and all the rags that he had gathered shined for cleanliness.

Well, then I lowered my head and trembling for all that I had seen, I myself walked up to the Ragman. I told him my name with shame, for I was a sorry figure next to him. Then I took off all my clothes in that place, and I said to him with dear yearning in my voice: "Dress me."

He dressed me. My Lord, he put new rags on me, and I am a wonder beside him. The Ragman, the Ragman, the Christ!

NOTES AND REFLECTIONS

January 2017

Sunday	Monday	Tuesday	Wednesday	Thursday	Friday	Saturday
1	2	3	4	5	6	7
8	9	10	11	12	13	14
15	16	17	18	19	20	21
22	23	24	25	26	27	28
29	30	31				

January

First Sunday

Life Verses

A co-worker shared his "life verse," and asked the group at a staff meeting what was their special verse. He had found his verse written on a barn shortly after he came to the Christian faith. I have to admit, I did not have a "life verse," but I shared what my husband's was from Psalm 51. However, a couple of important verses came to mind from my past, such as Matthew 11:28-30, when my life was much harder than it is today: "Come to Me, all you who are toiling and over-burdened, and I will give you relief. Take my yoke of submission upon you, and learn from Me, for I am gentle and humble in heart; and I will refresh your souls. For my yoke of submission is good, and My pack is light." I also thought of Isaiah 40:31 as a verse I clung to in the weariness of my life in the past: "But they who wait on the Lord shall renew their strength; they shall mount up with wings like eagles; they shall run and not be weary; they shall walk and not faint."

We all go through various seasons of life. Consider the changing seasons (winter, spring, summer, and autumn), and how God guides us through each of those seasons. As we live through autumn, we might be reminded of how quickly life can change, sometimes through sickness or death, or the unexpected loss of a job. We can watch the beauty of the color of the leaves change. We can also watch them die and fall to the ground, which sometimes leaves us with the feeling of empty, grey, cool days.

Then we approach winter, where we experience the quiet, cold, snowy nights that sometimes cause us to feel the distance or silence of God during times of trouble. By faith we know God never leaves us or forsakes us, but in times of crisis when we call out to Him, there are indeed times, if we are honest, that we cannot hear Him or find Him, and we feel alone.

Next comes spring, where life is in full bloom, the flowers start to grow, the buds on the trees burst forth, and we feel alive. Maybe we experience the birth of a baby, or a marriage, or a breakthrough in employment, or health restored, and we sense God's goodness, mercy and love.

Finally summer comes, where we may bask in the warmth and light of God's presence and all seems right with the world. Our relationships are good, our families are healthy, our finances are in order, and we feel blessed.

Of course, life does not come to us in these neat cycles, but the cycles of nature can remind us of how life changes, even though God does not. God is the same yesterday, today and forever; "For I the Lord do not change" (Malachi 3:6).

Now I reconsider my "life verse." I think of Ecclesiastes 3:1 which says, "For everything there is a season, and a time for every purpose under heaven." Perhaps you have a "life verse" but maybe you do not. The important thing is that we stay in God's Word and hold on to our faith through the various seasons of life, knowing God does not change, even when life does.

As you meditate this week on Scripture, perhaps you will find your "life verse," or contemplate your existing life verse and how God speaks through His Word in each season of your life.

NOTES AND REFLECTIONS

JANUARY

SECOND SUNDAY

Humility

Many have nativity scenes set up for Christmas that have recently been taken down and put away until next year. At church last week we laughed as we wondered how the three wise men ever got into our nativity sets. Of course, we have Mary and Joseph and baby Jesus, and usually have a shepherd boy with a little lamb around his shoulders, maybe a cow and sheep and an angel for the top of the manger; but we also have three wise men, astrologers from the East who are also in the manger scene.

From the reading of Scripture, we know the wise men (Magi) were not at the manger, but came to the house of Mary and Joseph, probably many months or perhaps even years after Jesus was born, since it would have taken them a long time to travel to where Jesus and his family lived. In the Gospel of Matthew, it was recorded, "After hearing the king's instructions, they (the Magi) departed; and the star in the east, went before them, until it stopped above the place where the young child was. When they saw the star, they were overwhelmed with intense joy. And when they reached the dwelling, they saw the young child with Mary His mother, and fell down to pay homage to Him; and when they had opened their treasures, they presented to Him gifts; gold, and frankincense, and myrrh" (Matthew 2:9-11).

Jesus was born in a manger to a teenage girl, who, along with Joseph, had nowhere to go to give birth. The only place available was a smelly place with animals where a stranger allowed them to stay, hardly the place for a King to be born. Yet the Magi, the wise astrologers from the East, gave Jesus the kingly gifts of gold, frankincense, which was offered on an incense altar in both the first and second Temples and also a symbol of a divine name (Malachi 1:11 and Song of Solomon 1:3), and myrrh, which was used for burials, foretelling Jesus' sacrificial death. These wise men (however many there were, we do not know), came to worship, for they knew Jesus was some kind of King, and they refused to report back to King Herod where Jesus lived, protecting Jesus from Herod's raging jealousy.

As Jesus grew, He probably learned the trade of "father" Joseph, and we know almost nothing about his childhood and young adulthood until about age thirty when He began His public ministry. Jesus, God in the flesh, remained poor and humble. He had no home of His own; "Jesus said, Foxes have holes and birds have nests; but the Son of Man has nowhere to lay His head" (Luke 9:58). Jesus did not come as the glorious King most people expected, but He came as a servant to mankind: "For the Son of man himself came not to be served, but to minister, and to give His life as a redemptive price for many" (Luke 10:45).

Jesus, who is the Word made flesh, who existed from the very beginning of time as Creator (John 1:-14), came quietly and humbly to serve His creation, to suffer and die for His people, and will surely come back one day as the triumphant King of glory. Yet during His lifetime,

Jesus remained humble, the "Suffering Servant" we read about in Isaiah 53; but even as Christians, how many of us struggle with pride? How many look at material possessions and wealth, or our educations and careers and think we have done well for ourselves and measure success by all we have accomplished? How many would be able to humble ourselves anywhere close to how Jesus chose to do? How many would choose to serve, rather than to be served?

This week, as you put the Christmas decorations away and pack away the nativity set remember Jesus, the King, who was presented with kingly gifts, but who chose humility and poverty, in order to serve His people. Should we not have that same attitude as Christ followers?

NOTES AND REFLECTIONS

JANUARY

THIRD SUNDAY

Brotherly Love

In mid-January we celebrate Martin Luther King Day. Dr. King was a powerful Christian minister who gave an eloquent speech in Washington D.C. on August 28, 1963 on the steps of the Lincoln Memorial: "I Have a Dream." There are many lines in that speech which reflect the teachings of Jesus and the Apostle Paul, of which Dr. King was familiar. One of the lines in Dr. King's famous speech was, "In the process of gaining our rightful place, we must not be guilty of wrongful deeds. Let us not seek to satisfy our thirst for freedom from drinking from the cup of bitterness and hatred." Dr. Martin Luther King Jr. also said in his speech, "I am not unmindful that some of you have come here out of great trials and tribulations. Some of you have come fresh from narrow jail cells. Some of you have come from areas where your quest for freedom left you battered by the storms of persecution and staggered by the winds of police brutality. You have been veterans of creative suffering. Continue to work with the faith that unearned suffering is redemptive."

Dr. King taught his congregation and the people involved in the Civil Rights Movement to follow the difficult words of Jesus and of St. Paul in Romans 12:12, 14, "Remain steadfast in times of trouble; be persistent in the habit of prayer... bless all who persecute you; bless and curse not." Again in Romans 12:17, 21, Paul wrote, "Never pay back injury for injury. Aim to do what is honorable in the sight of all men... Never permit evil to conquer you, but get the better of evil by doing good." Dr. King's words echoed Jesus' teachings in the Sermon on the Mount in Matthew 5 where Jesus spoke about retaliation: "You have heard that it was said, 'An eye for an eye and a tooth for a tooth'. But I say to you, Do not resist an evil doer, But if anyone strikes you on the right cheek, turn the other also" (Matthew 5:38-39). Again, Dr. King's speech reflected Jesus' teaching in Matthew 5:43-44: "You have heard that it was said, 'You shall love your neighbor and hate your enemy.' But I say to you, Love your enemies and pray for those who persecute you."

Dr. Martin Luther King and the Civil Rights Movement used the principles of Scripture to overcome evil with good, and with the assistance and power of God, they began to do good work in this country. Many probably would not have the courage and the forgiveness that Martin Luther King and many of his followers displayed during that period. We can be grateful this man led a movement based on the teachings of Scripture and as Christians, brothers and sisters in Christ, no matter what the color or ethnicity, should also use the principles of Scripture daily in our own lives.

This week, take a moment to remember Dr. Martin Luther King Jr., and thank God for him and the brothers and sisters who truly lived out the teachings of Scripture, as we seek to do the same. Pray for God's love and strength to enable us to walk in the infinite love of our Savior and Redeemer, Jesus Christ.

NOTES AND REFLECTIONS

JANUARY
FOURTH SUNDAY

The Sanctity of Life

In America each January, many Christians celebrate the Sanctity of Life Sunday. January 22, is the March for Life in Washington D.C., marking the anniversary of Roe vs. Wade, the legalization of abortion in America. As someone who has been to the March For Life in Washington many times, and as someone who was a single parent for 34 years, I understand God's love and provision for all children, whether they were humanly planned or not. God plans all life and loves all life. God is the Author and giver of life. God loves each unborn child. As Christians, we know that life is precious and a marvelous gift from God.

Many know the Scripture in Jeremiah 1:4-5, "Now the word of the Lord came to me saying, Before I formed you in the womb I knew you, and before you were born I consecrated you." God loves us all and has a plan for our lives even before we are born. In Psalm 139:13&16, King David wrote, "For it was you who formed my inward parts; you knit me together in my mother's womb. I praise you, for I am fearfully and wonderfully made...Your eyes beheld my unformed substance. In your book were written all the days that were formed for me, when none of them as yet existed." Isaiah also wrote, "The Lord called me before I was born, while I was in my mother's womb he named me" (Isaiah 49:1 b).

When Mary, the Mother of Jesus was pregnant, she went to visit her aunt Elizabeth, who was also pregnant with John the Baptist. Scripture records, "In the days that followed, Mary rose up and hastened to the hill country, to a city of Judah; and entered the house of Zacharias and greeted Elizabeth. As soon as Elizabeth heard Mary's greeting, the unborn child jumped in her womb; and Elizabeth was filled with the Holy Spirit" (Luke 1:39-41). While in the womb, John was excited about Jesus, who was also in the womb!

We have life before we are born and are precious to God. Many women may not have fully understood or even known those Scriptures that speak of life in the womb, which are already known by God, and perhaps have ended their pregnancy. We know God abundantly loves and He will forgive and heal when asked with repentance. We serve an amazingly merciful God.

This month many will converge on Washington, D. C. to pray for the unborn and for the sanctity of all life, please keep them in prayer. And remember always to show love, to those who agree with us on the sanctity of life, and to those who disagree. Thank God that He is mindful, loving, and merciful - even before we were born.

NOTES AND REFLECTIONS

JANUARY
FIFTH SUNDAY

Through the Eyes of Christ

When we are converted to Christianity, the Holy Spirit indwells us, and we become new people. We begin to see the world from a different perspective; we should also start to see people differently. St Paul wrote in Galatians 2:20, "I was crucified with Christ; nevertheless I live, yet not I, but Christ lives in me; and the life I live now in the flesh I live by the faith of the Son of God, who loved me and gave Himself for me." We are to crucify continually the old nature, the old ways of doing things, the old attitudes, and allow the power of the Holy Spirit to live through us as new creations. We need to ask Jesus daily to allow us to see others as He sees them. Paul wrote to the Philippian Christians, "Let your dispositions and thoughts be the same as Christ Jesus" (Philippians 2:5). To have the mind of Christ, though, is a process of personal sanctification that only God can work in us.

Eric Scalise, Ph.D., Vice President for Professional Development with the American Association of Christian Counselors has several interesting thoughts on how differently we may see people, as opposed to the viewpoint of Jesus. Dr. Scalise said in a training DVD for the Light University, "The world sees only that a man is dying from AIDS and whispers, 'he probably deserves that,' but Jesus sees someone who is alone and afraid of dying. The world sees only the alcoholic lost and groping in darkness, but Jesus sees someone whose life can be restored. The world sees only the woman who is always anxious and depressed, but Jesus sees the single mom struggling to survive and needing the support and understanding of others. The world sees only the 'throwaways' in prison, the crippled, the poor, the homeless, but Jesus sees precious souls that have yet to be invited to the banquet table. The world sees only the prostitute standing on the corner, but Jesus sees the little girl who was sexually abused and desperate for a father's love. The world sees only the rebellious teenager wanting to end his or her life, but Jesus sees someone who has never been accepted and starving for approval. The world saw only a robber crucified as a common thief, but Jesus saw a lost soul worth dying for."

When Paul wrote to the Corinthian church that, "If any man be in Christ, he is a new creation; observe, the old things have passed away; all things become new" (2 Corinthians 5:17) he was not only referring to what we do, but also our attitudes and how we think. If we are Christ's hands and feet here on earth, we must see and love people in the same way He does. It is wonderful to work in an environment where people do indeed see others through the eyes of Christ, but it is also a good idea to be reminded each day to love and view others (including ourselves), as Christ sees people, His crowning creation. Thank God He can indeed make us a new creation through His grace and mercy.

This week, as you encounter various people from all walks of life, pray that the Holy Spirit will enable you to see others as Christ sees them, not how the natural, human nature sometimes views people who are different from others, and to love them as Christ does.

NOTES AND REFLECTIONS

February 2017

Sunday	Monday	Tuesday	Wednesday	Thursday	Friday	Saturday
			1	2	3	4
5	6	7	8	9	10	11
12	13	14	15	16	17	18
19	20	21	22	23	24	25
26	27	28				

FEBRUARY
FIRST SUNDAY

Forgiveness and the Lord's Prayer

Most of us pray the Lord's Prayer; some recite this prayer every Sunday in church worship services. There is one line in this beautiful prayer that if we honestly and deeply considered: "and forgive us our trespasses as we forgive those who trespass against us" (Matthew 6:12 NRSV) would change our lives. When we pray this section of the Lord's Prayer, and ask God to forgive us in the same manner that we forgive others, do we realize what we are asking God to do? What if we are holding a grudge and not forgiving someone, perhaps someone who has hurt us deeply? We are literally asking God NOT to forgive us! Imagine that?

Also, the verses directly following the Lord's Prayer say, "For if you forgive others their trespasses, your heavenly Father will also forgive you; but if you do not forgive others, neither will your Father forgive your trespasses" (Matthew 6:14-15, New Revised Standard Version). I don't know about you, but those words of Jesus about not forgiving others cause me to reconsider my own heart.

Forgiveness is spoken of many times in the Bible. Salvation depends on God's grace and forgiveness for our own sins. Matthew 18:21-22 recounted a question Peter asked Jesus: "Then came Peter to Jesus, and asked, Lord, how often shall I forgive my brother who sins against me? Would seven times be enough?' Jesus answered, I say not, until seven times: but until seventy-seven times." In other words, forgiveness is beyond calculating and there is no record keeping system.

In the Beatitudes in Matthew 5:7, Jesus said, "Blessed are the merciful, for they shall receive mercy." Jesus also said in Matthew 5:11, "Blessed are you when people revile you and persecute you and utter all kinds of evil against you falsely on my account. Rejoice and be glad, for your reward is great in Heaven" (both references taken from the New Revised Standard version).

These preceding verses in Scripture make me think of Corrie Ten Boom, a Holocaust survivor, whose family was killed in that terrible genocide, while she survived the brutal death camps. One day, many years after her release from the camps, she saw one of the Nazi torturers who had brutalized her, as he spoke at a church service she attended. He had become a Christian and was giving his testimony. Corrie Ten Boom said she listened to him with anger and hatred, remembering all of the terrible things she experienced at his hand. When he had finished speaking, and as everyone was leaving the church, Corrie went and shook his hand. She wondered how she could possibly shake this man's hand, though she knew she must, with a forgiving heart.

When she approached the former Nazi Guard, she prayed that God would enable her simply to lift her arm to touch him, because she could not do so on her own. God, of course, did give her the strength to do so, and she said as her hand touched his, her hatred and unforgiving spirit just melted away. She knew God was at work. Corrie Ten Boom quoted Mother Teresa who once said, "People are illogical, unreasonable, and self-centered. Love them anyway." If she was able to forgive such cruelty, surely we can forgive others as well. Jesus commands us to forgive, and with the help of His Holy Spirit, we can too.

Let me leave you this week with an interesting quote from Mahatma Gandhi; "The weak can never forgive. Forgiveness is an attribute of the strong." Are we not strong through Christ Jesus who strengthens us? "I can do all things through Christ who provides me strength" (Philippians 4:13). May you have a loving and mercy-filled week, and as you pray the Lord's Prayer this week, meditate on forgiveness, and ask God to show you where you may still have some bitterness and unforgiveness, and may God give you a heart that forgives.

NOTES AND REFLECTIONS

FEBRUARY

SECOND SUNDAY

The Greatest Commandment

Some know what Jesus told the Scribes and Pharisees when they asked Him what "the greatest commandment" was from the Gospels. "And one of the scribes came, and having heard the discussion, perceived that Jesus had answered admirably, asked, Which of the commandments is in first position? And Jesus answered, The chief one is, Hear, O Israel; The Lord your God is one Lord; And thou shall love the Lord your God with your whole heart, and with your whole existence, and with all your moral understanding, and with all your ability and strength: namely this, You shall love as yourself those near you. There is no other commandment greater than these" (Mark 12:28-31).

We may also be familiar with the lawyer in the Gospel of Luke, who asked Jesus how to inherit eternal life: "Teacher, what shall I do to inherit eternal life? He answered, What is written in the text? How do you read it?' He answered, You shall love the Lord your God continually with your whole heart, and with your whole soul, and with your whole strength, and with your whole mind; and your neighbor as your own self. Jesus said that is correct: do this, and you shall live. And he, willing to justify himself, said to Jesus, And who is my neighbor?" (Luke 10:25-28).

From there, Jesus proceeded to tell the parable of the Good Samaritan... our neighbor is everyone, including those we do not particularly care for, and even our enemies. We know the Jews did not associate with the Samaritans and did not like them at all, but Jesus told the lawyer (and us!), that we are to love them anyway.

Sometimes it is hard enough to truly love the people in our own families, churches, workplace, and circle of friends, or some with whom we may not normally associate. Do we truly love each and every person we meet and know? Sometimes we may simply try to show kindness and try to be polite, but we may not truly feel love for all people as Jesus taught. I heard someone once say, "We need the presence of righteousness, not just the absence of sin." As Christians, it is not enough simply to be polite or not be unkind to others; we also must truly love.

Martin Luther wrote in his Large Catechism that "if loving God and our neighbor is the greatest commandment, then not loving God and our neighbor as ourselves must be the greatest sin!" Luther's statement makes logical sense.

This week, as you think about the "Greatest Commandment," the commandment in the first position, you may also want to review the "love chapter" in the Bible to meditate on, and pray about putting these verses into your daily life: "Love is long-suffering and sympathetic; love has no jealousy, love is not anxious to impress others, does not hold inflated ideas of self-importance, has good manners, is not self-seeking, is never provoked, does not keep score of wrongs; takes no pleasure in wrongdoing, but rejoices when truth is victorious; there is no limit to endurance, love has endless faith and great expectations, there is no end to love's tolerance" (1 Cor. 13:4-7).

NOTES AND REFLECTIONS

February

Third Sunday

The Impossible

At the 2015 Global Missions Health Conference in Louisville, Kentucky, an American missionary named Joseph spoke about his life as a medical missionary in the African Republic of Congo. Joseph worked and lived in the Congo with his wife and children, and had done so for many years. He said at eight years old he knew and wanted to be a missionary, but was unsure of what type of work he wanted to do. When he was getting failing grades in penmanship, his mother jokingly suggested he should be a doctor since she said most doctors seem to have ineligible handwriting, which is what he became. It is often quite humorous how God sometimes chooses to reveal His will!

Congo's Pioneer Christian Hospital opened its doors in January 2006, where Joseph worked. The hospital, formerly a Communist youth camp, now was a place of health, healing, and hope. The hospital provides all types of medical services and a chaplaincy program. It is amazing how God can transform the bad into good! God changed a place of hate and suffering into a place of love and healing. God can do the same thing in broken lives and circumstances; the seemingly impossible is really God's work!

Think about the drastic conversion of Saul/Paul as recounted in Acts 9: "And Saul still breathing hard with aggressive and murderous desire against the disciples of the Lord approached the high priest and asked for letters addressed to the synagogues in Damascus, so that if he found any men or women of the Way he might bring them bound to Jerusalem" (Acts 9:1-2). Along the way, Jesus spoke to Saul and asked, "Why do you persecute Me?" (Acts 9:4). Saul had an encounter with Jesus that changed him forever, and at that point in time, Saul, the persecutor and hater of Christians, became Paul a lover of Christ and His Church. Mark 10:27 records, "For with God all things are possible."

We look at the world around us, filled with so much hate and violence that it is hard to conceptualize the reality of evil. We look around at some people who are confused, troubled, addicted, hateful, bitter or angry, and wonder where God can be in their lives and in their world. We meet people in this condition every day, but they, too, can have the same Damascus Road experience as the Apostle Paul. We should pray for the "impossible" - the conversion of the troubled all over the world, including right here in our own neighborhood or family. Since God can turn a Communist youth camp into a Christian Hospital, and can convert the hateful Saul into the Apostle Paul, a loving follower of Jesus Christ, and since He turned our own lives around, we know that truly nothing is impossible with God.

This week, may God provide the faith to believe that with each day, and with each person we meet, He can turn all things around for His purpose and for His glory, and do what men think impossible.

NOTES AND REFLECTIONS

FEBRUARY

FOURTH SUNDAY

Ash Wednesday

Six weeks before Easter, we celebrate Ash Wednesday, which is the first day of Lent. Not all Christians celebrate this season of the Church calendar, though it has a long history in Western Christianity dating back to the late eighth century. Ash Wednesday is a Day of Fasting, and is 46 days before Easter Sunday. The Lenten Fast is from Monday-Saturday, beginning with Ash Wednesday, but does not include Sundays since the Resurrection of Jesus Christ is commemorated on Sundays during this six week Lenten Season. Sundays are Feast Days, and not a time to fast. In the Gospels, we see this practice of fasting and feasting; Jesus was asked, "Why do John's disciples and the Pharisees fast often and make prayers, and your disciples eat and drink? And He said, Can you cause the attendants of the bridegroom to fast while the bridegroom is present? And the days will come when the bridegroom is taken away violently, then shall they fast" (Luke 5:33-35).

The Lenten Fast is broken on Easter Sunday, when the Resurrection of Jesus is celebrated. Lent lasts for 40 days, representing the 40-day-fast that Jesus spent in the wilderness when He was tempted by Satan, as recorded in Matthew 4. During Lent, Christians are called to contemplate their sinful nature and to use this time as a season of repentance. We know Jesus was tempted but never sinned: "We can claim a great high priest, Jesus, the Son of God, who has ascended into heaven, therefore, let us hold fast the faith we profess. For we have a high priest who can lay a hand on our personal feebleness, because He has gone through every temptation, just the same way we have, and remains without sin" (Hebrews 4:14,15).

Ash Wednesday gives Believers 40 days to prepare for Easter, contemplating the life and death of our Lord and Savior Jesus Christ, as we prepare for Good Friday and Easter Sunday. The 40 day fast of Lent can take many different forms. Some people give up some pleasure they normally indulge in, such as sweets, or meat, or they may fast a meal or two each day. Some people also focus on adding additional worship services to their week and may attend a mid-week service in addition to the regular Sunday service, to prepare their hearts and minds for The Passion of Christ.

In many Christian denominations, people will receive the imposition of ashes from their priest or minister. The ashes come from the burnt palm branches from the previous year's Palm Sunday celebration, and are placed in the sign of a cross on a person's forehead, as the minister says either, "Repent and believe in the Gospel," or, "Remember that you are dust, and to dust you shall return" taken from Genesis 3:19 which God told Adam and Eve after their Fall. In the Bible, repentance usually involved the penitent sinner wearing sackcloth and sprinkling ashes over his or her head, which is why ashes are placed on the foreheads of the Christians during this season.

Whether or not you are a Christian who observes Ash Wednesday and practices a Lenten Fast, remember the Great High Priest, Jesus, who endured a 40 day fast, was tempted, yet was without sin. Jesus died in our place, because when tempted, we all have sinned, and we are born with a sinful nature. Jesus took on all the sins of the world, but He was raised to conquer death for all time, and came to give us eternal, glorious life with Him.

NOTES AND REFLECTIONS

March 2017

Sunday	Monday	Tuesday	Wednesday	Thursday	Friday	Saturday
			1	2	3	4
5	6	7	8	9	10	11
12	13	14	15	16	17	18
19	20	21	22	23	24	25
26	27	28	29	30	31	

MARCH

FIRST SUNDAY

The Privilege of Suffering

We live in a time of terror, fear, violence, and suffering. We see Christians being killed for their faith, along with other innocent people, and at times we cannot help but perhaps wonder why... Where is God in the midst of all this turmoil, destruction, and suffering? As Christians, we know that Christ is right there in the middle of the suffering, and we know that God is ultimately in control of this universe, yet our hearts still melt in sadness and our minds perhaps in bewilderment at the news we hear and see each day. What does the Bible teach us about suffering? We know that Christ suffered more than any of us will ever suffer, since He not only suffered the betrayal of friends and the physical torture of His beatings and crucifixion, but more importantly, He took on all the sins of the world that have ever and will ever be committed.

In 2 Corinthians 11, the Apostle Paul spoke of imprisonments, countless floggings, stoning's, shipwrecks, dangers from bandits, from Gentiles, even from his own people, dangers from wild animals, and he experienced hunger, thirst, and exposure to harsh elements, yet he viewed his sufferings as a privilege. Paul wrote in Philippians 1:29, "For you were granted on behalf of Christ, the privilege not only to believe on Him, but also to suffer for His sake." Amazing! Who among us considers it a privilege to suffer?

A missionary named Deborah, recently told a story about her work in various parts of Asia and Africa. She worked as a nurse and was kidnapped and held hostage in Eritrea with another nurse friend. Deborah was pregnant at that time and was praying that her husband, friends, and the mission organization in which they worked would be able to pay her ransom to gain her freedom. One day during their hostage situation, she and her nurse friend were told to run across a field, so arm and arm they ran; suddenly, her friend fell to the ground - shot dead. In fear and shock, Deborah kept running, until there was nowhere else to run, and then she was beaten by her captors. Deborah said that through her tears and fears, all she could do was follow God through this suffering, knowing God is present always, especially in the midst of suffering. Deborah said she never lost her faith, and upon her release, she remained a missionary for many more years; she did not give up. Her baby was even born healthy! This amazing missionary even said that she felt it was a privilege to suffer, knowing Jesus suffered so much more, and that He was so very close to her in the midst of her suffering.

In whatever way we may suffer through life, this faithful missionary nurse, like the apostle Paul, said it is a privilege to suffer for Christ, for it is during these times that we are so aware of the presence of God. Paul also wrote that in times of suffering, "God said, my grace is sufficient for you: for my strength is made perfect in weakness" (2 Cor. 12:9). God works in powerful ways through our suffering.

May we always know God's presence with each day, by faith, but especially in times of suffering, or as we watch others suffer. This week, let us pray for God's enduring presence in this fragile and uncertain time in which we live, and when we suffer, may we draw closer to God and abide in His loving presence.

NOTES AND REFLECTIONS

MARCH

SECOND SUNDAY

Persistence in Prayer

Have you ever prayed for something, persistently and fervently prayed for something, day in and day out, only to feel like your prayers "fell on deaf ears" and God was just not listening? If you have felt this, you are not alone. Psalm 10:1 says, "Why, O Lord, do you stand far away? Why do you hide yourself in times of trouble?"

I have a family member who had been praying for something for years, for something very good and for what seemed like it would be God's perfect and loving will, but the exact opposite of her prayer is what recently happened. She said to me, "God must not be listening, or He is simply punishing me for some reason after all the praying I've been doing and the way this worked out." Of course we know in our head that statement is not true, and that "God's ways are not our ways," but even some of the prophets and great biblical men and women of God sometimes felt that same way.

The Old Testament prophet Habakkuk is someone to whom I can relate. He quite openly complained to God that He was silent, that He was not listening to his cries for justice, and Habakkuk could not at all understand what God was doing in the very violent and turbulent time in which he lived. At the very beginning of the book, Habakkuk said,

"Lord, how long shall I cry for help, and you will not listen?" (Habakkuk 1:2).

All of us at some time in our lives have or will feel the way Habakkuk (and my family member) did. We pray for work, for health, for relationships or for whatever are desperate needs in our life, and sometimes God appears silent or just not listening. But God said to Habakkuk, "A work is being done in your days that you would not believe if you were told" (Hab. 1:5 b). God is always at work in our lives, and we probably would not believe what He is doing, even if He did indeed come down and tell us (which I know many of us sometimes wish He would do). What amazes me, in the book of Habakkuk, is that God actually took the time to reply to this prophet. God does not owe us an explanation, yet the dialogue continues throughout this book.

The Apostle Paul quoted Habakkuk 2:4 b in Romans 1:17 when he wrote, "The just live by faith," and Paul also wrote in II Corinthians 5:7, "For we walk by faith and not by vision."

There are times, many times, when faith can be a very difficult part of our walk with Christ. So often we simply cannot understand what God is doing. I have an old pastor friend who once said to me that if we could understand God, He would cease to be God; He would simply be like us. But do we want a God like us, especially when we contemplate our mistakes, our frailties, our sins and all the times we are wrong?

The prophet Habakkuk ends his book on a beautiful note of confidence in the Lord, when he wrote, "Though the fig tree does not blossom, and no fruit is on the vines; though the produce of the olive fails, and the fields yield no food; though the flock is cut off from the fold, and there is no herd in the stalls, yet I will rejoice in the Lord; I will exult in the God of my salvation" (Habakkuk. 3:17-18).

We serve a mighty God who is always at work in this world and in our lives to bring about His glory and His perfect will, even when we do not understand. Meditate on the book of Habakkuk this week, and remember that when God seems to be silent or does not appear to hear your prayers, in faith we can know that God is always doing a good work in our lives.

NOTES AND REFLECTIONS

MARCH

THIRD SUNDAY

Uncertainty and Confusion

Due to various circumstances, we come to a crossroad where we must make some tough decisions: do we remain where we are living, working, worshipping, etc., or is God calling us to move on? Do we change careers, go back to school, leave the mission field...there are a number of scenarios we can face during our lives. In Hebrew, a fork-in-the-road (crossroad) is called literally "an opening of the eyes." Many years ago, I was in that position. I had just graduated from seminary, closed a successful business, sold my house and moved to another state, away from friends and family and the security I had known. Some people questioned this decision, and over the years, at times, I had as well, especially when things did not turn out as planned; however, in my heart and mind I knew this was the direction God was calling me, even when life did not make sense.

Thomas Merton, a Trappist monk who lived at Gethsemani for twenty-seven years in Kentucky, wrote a prayer that spoke of our occasional confusion and uncertainties. He wrote, "My Lord God, I have no idea where I am going. I do not see the road ahead of me. I cannot know for certain where it will end. Nor do I really know myself, and the fact that I think I am following your will does not mean that I am actually doing so. But I believe that the desire to please you does in fact please you. And I hope I have that desire in all that I am doing. I hope I will never do anything apart from that desire. And I know that if I do this you will lead me by the right road, though I may know nothing about it..."

God will reveal His plans for our lives when we seek Him, but the outcome is often unknown or different from what we expected. It may be difficult at times to determine God's will, but Scripture is the best place to turn, especially when we hear many different voices telling us many different things. If any of our plans are not in accordance with the Word of God, they are not of Him. If our decisions are based on God's Truth and we have peace, God will guide and direct our steps. I have also learned that God can also use plan B if we made an honest, faithful mistake, and use it for His glory!

A friend of mine once said to me, "When we come to the edge of the light that we know, and are about to step off into the unknown, of this we can be sure...either God will provide something solid to stand on, or we will be taught to fly." Take a step, or a flight of faith, where God will enable us to fly on eagles wings. "But they who wait on the Lord shall renew their strength; they shall mount up with wings as eagles; they shall run and not be weary; they shall walk and not faint."(Isaiah 40:31).

NOTES AND REFLECTIONS

MARCH

FOURTH SUNDAY

The Faith of a Child

When I was a young child, I did something many children do: I stood on about the third stair inside our home that led to the second floor, and then simply fell, knowing my mother would catch me as she stood at the bottom of the stairs. I remember mother saying to me, "You have no doubt I will catch you!" As a young girl, I knew my mother did not want me to get hurt, and I knew that yes, she would indeed catch me as I fell into her arms. Jesus said, "Permit the children to come to Me, and do not hinder them: for of such is the kingdom of God. Truly I say, Whoever shall not welcome the kingdom of God as a little child shall in no wise enter therein" (Luke 18:16-17). What is it about children that Jesus spoke about that we lose as adults? We lose that pure, innocent trust and faith, the kind of faith that causes us to jump from stairs into someone's arms.

In a recent sermon, my pastor, Jim Bettermann, spoke about the faith of a child. He said that when (most American) children go to bed, they know their parents are in the next room looking after them and will keep them safe through the night. Children know when they wake up in the morning they will have food on the table, and when they come home from school, their parents will be there and they will once again have food on the table. They know they will have clothes to wear and water to drink. Children do not worry, but they trust their parents to care for them. (I realize these circumstances are not true all over the world, especially in worn-torn countries and impoverished countries with many orphans and street children), but when we think of our own children and grandchildren, they do have a simple, child-like trust that we lose as we grow old. As an aging adult, I'm not so sure I would completely trust someone to catch me anymore!

Jesus told us we are to have that same trust in Him as our Heavenly Father, and that we can figuratively throw ourselves into His waiting arms as well, knowing He will catch us and not let us fall. That does not mean that we can act recklessly, foolishly, or sinfully, and put God to the test, but it does mean we can have the faith of a child to know that our Heavenly Father watches over us and guides us in the path He wants us to go. When we follow His path, He will walk beside us and keep us from stumbling as we depend on Him. But why do we still worry about so many things? What do you worry about: Your children or grandchildren; your health; your job; your finances; your safety? "And Jesus said to His disciples; Therefore, I say to you, stop worrying about your life, what you will eat; neither about clothes for the body. Consider the ravens: for they neither sow nor reap; they neither have storehouse nor barn: and God feeds them: how much more are you better than the ravens?" (Luke 12:22-24). Jesus is calling us to a child-like faith.

As a young child, I never worried about anything. I trusted my parents would be home with me in the evenings, that I would have dinner to eat each night, that I had a safe home to sleep in, and that there would be something to eat in the morning. In the Gospel of Luke we read, "If a son asks bread of his father, will he give him a stone? Or if he asks for a fish, will he give him a serpent? Or if he asks for an egg, will he give him a scorpion? If you then, being human, provide good gifts for your children: how much more will your heavenly Father give the gift of the Holy Spirit to those who ask him?" (Luke 11:11-13).

If you are a parent or grandparent, would you not be upset if your child or grandchild told you they did not trust you to care for them and doubted your love for them? How much more our Father in Heaven loves and cares for us, and desires our faith and trust in His love, protection and care. This week, let us all pray for the faith of a child, and to be willing to jump off the steps of life in to the arms of our strong, loving and waiting Father.

NOTES AND REFLECTIONS

April 2017

Sunday	Monday	Tuesday	Wednesday	Thursday	Friday	Saturday
						1
2	3	4	5	6	7	8
9	10	11	12	13	14	15
16	17	18	19	20	21	22
23 30	24	25	26	27	28	29

APRIL

FIRST SUNDAY

Palm Sunday

Shortly before the Passover celebration, a great crowd of people gathered in excitement: "On the next day many who were attending the feast, heard that Jesus was coming to Jerusalem, and took palm branches and went out to meet Jesus, and cried, Hosanna: Blessed is the King of Israel who comes in the Name of the Lord" (John 12:12-13).

These people, who were so excited about Jesus, had heard of His many miracles, including the raising of Lazarus from the dead. They came out to see this miracle-worker, as well as the man He raised from the dead, Lazarus; but their enthusiasm did not last long; not even a week! Were they any different than us?

When we see great things that God does, or when He answers an urgent prayer, we are excited and give great praise to God shouting our own brand of Hosanna's. The big question is how do we react in the more difficult or even the more mundane times? Are we still so enthusiastic about our faith? Do we still shout Hosanna when God appears silent or distant? What about when we experience great heartache or loss? Do we still wave our palm branches, and shout great praises to the King? Jesus addressed this issue in one of His parables – the parable of the sower found in

Mark 4 (also found in Matthew and Luke), which reminds me of the short-lived enthusiasm on that first Palm Sunday.

In the parable of the sower, the seed that is sown on the ground is the word of God – the Gospel. Some of the people heard the word of God, but their seed was "sown on stony ground; who, when they heard the word, immediately received it with gladness; but they had no real roots, and so endured for a short time: afterward, when affliction or persecution came for the word's sake, they were easily hurt" and they fell away (Mark 4:16-17). In other words, when life becomes challenging or painful, there are no more palm branches waving, no more Hosanna's being shouted, and the excitement is gone, maybe to the point of even turning our backs on Jesus and denying Him.

By contrast, Jesus demands that His disciples, His children, follow Him in good times and in bad – in ALL times, even taking up the Cross and following Him to Golgotha where He was crucified. Jesus requires us to remain faithful to Him, to shout praises to Him, even as we walk the Via Dolorosa, the road of suffering. Palm Sunday must continue all year long, and not just for a few inspiring and exciting days. Palm Sunday follows Jesus all the way to His death, knowing Easter is coming. "Hold on, Easter is coming!" is sometimes all we can say.

This week, as we approach Palm Sunday, and we see Jesus, the King and miracle worker, let us remember to wave our palm branches and shout praises to Him not just this week, but through Good Friday, knowing Easter is coming!

NOTES AND REFLECTIONS

APRIL

SECOND SUNDAY

The Women

"Good Friday," was anything but good for Jesus. It was an excruciating, painful, lonely, horribly dark day. Jesus hung, dying on the Cross to pay in full the penalty for the sins of the world. Scripture told us many women were there, having followed Jesus from Galilee to care for His needs. Mark 15:40-41 records, "There were also many women looking on from a distance: among them were Mary Magdalene, and Mary, the mother of the younger James, and Mary the mother of Joseph, and Salome; (Who also, when He was in Galilee, followed Him, and ministered to Him;) and many other women that came up with Him to Jerusalem." Symbolically, there is great theological significance surrounding these women. In the ancient eastern world, kings traveled with many women who were their aides and attendants, who were there to care for the king's needs, and who were always in the king's immediate presence. If we appreciated today, as well as the people who lived in Jesus' day, understood Jesus to be King, they would have recognized the significance of the many women who traveled with Jesus and cared for His needs.

The Gospel recorded in Mark 14:3-9 something that Jesus saw as a beautiful act from a woman, "And being in Bethany in the house of Simon the leper, as He reclined

at table, a woman came having a perfume vial of precious
ointment made from a rare plant (nard); and she broke
the vial, and poured it on his head. Some present were
indignant about this, and said, Why this waste of precious
ointment made? It could have been sold for more than three
hundred pieces of silver, and given to the poor. And they
murmured against her. And Jesus said, Let her alone; why
trouble her? She has done a worthy deed for Me. For you
have the poor with you always, and whenever you wish you
may do them good: but Me you will not always have. She
has done what she could: she has come before My death
to anoint My body for burial. This is the truth, wherever
this gospel is preached throughout the whole world, what
she has done will be spoken of as a memorial of her." Once
again, there was a humble woman meeting the needs of a
King.

Many women financially supported Jesus as He
traveled with His disciples, meeting Jesus the King's
material needs. "Then Jesus traveled from city to village and
preached and showed the good news of the kingdom of God:
and the Twelve were with Him. And women, who had been
healed of evil spirits and infirmities, Mary called Magdalene,
out of whom He expelled seven demons, and Joanna, the
wife of Chuza, Herod's steward, and Susanna, and many
others, who supported Him with personal resources." (Luke
8:1-3). It was also women who went to attend to the body of
Jesus when they thought He was still lying in the tomb. "At
first light on the first day of the week, the women and some
others came to the tomb, bringing prepared spices."(Luke
24:1)

Women played an important role in caring for King
Jesus while He was alive, and even attempted to care for

His body after He was Crucified. Jesus was then, and truly is now, King of Kings and Lord of Lords. When Jesus was being tried before the Jews, Pilate even said to the people, "Behold, your King!" (John 19:14). The sign above Jesus' head on the Cross, which listed the "crime" for which He was crucified read, THE KING OF THE JEWS (Mark 15:26). Jesus was not only the King of the Jews, but was and is the King of all people and all of Creation.

This week, as we celebrate Holy Week, remember to think about Jesus not only as our Savior, but more importantly, as our Lord and King. If you read Scripture carefully, knowing some of the history of the ancient eastern kings and how women took care of them, remember to view Jesus as the King of all His creation, and most importantly, as the King of our lives. (Credit to Joshua Collins for much of his theological insight in this devotion).

NOTES AND REFLECTIONS

APRIL

THIRD SUNDAY

Life and Death

April is the month when we begin to see new life burst forth after a cold, dark winter where the trees and plants were dormant and seemingly dead. We longed for the warmth, beauty and life of the new season. At some point, we dealt with the reality of human mortality; and, if we live long enough, we will all experience the death and bereavement of people we love. However, we should consider, to a much greater degree, the eternal significance of spiritual life and death. "I call Heaven and earth to witness against you today that I have set before you, life and death, blessings and curses. Choose life so that you and your descendants may live, loving the Lord your God, obeying Him, and holding fast to Him." (Deuteronomy 30:19, 20).

As Christ followers, we have the wonderful opportunity of sharing the blessed life of joyful obedience to our Heavenly Father who sent Jesus to give us true life. In John 10:10, Jesus said, "I am come that they may have life, and have it abundantly." How truly blessed we are to have such a loving God who offers us life - abundant life, and to give us the awesome joy of sharing that life with all those we come in contact with each day. Through the help of the Holy Spirit, we can indeed choose life! As recorded in the Gospel of John, Jesus said, "Truly, I say, He that hears My Word, and believes on Him who sent Me, has everlasting life, and will not face judgement; but has passed from death to life" (John 5:24). In Christ, we truly do have life!

Two women came to see me one afternoon at the rescue mission, and both told me they felt like they had "lost their souls" through the pains and difficulties of life, and they did not know how to "get it back," meaning their souls! They said they felt dead inside; they no longer really felt alive. Neither of these women knew of the abundant life that was available to them in Christ. What a joy to share the love of Jesus with them and to ensure them that God holds each soul tightly in His love, and continues to pursue us in order to share His grace, love and mercy, which truly does flood our souls. The Good Shepherd, "keeps watch over our souls" (1 Peter 2:25). Since God guards our souls and gives us abundant life, even when life is painful and difficult, we can rest assured that God will burst forth life into our souls, even when they feel cold, brown and dried up like a winter tree. Instead of choosing death, the Holy Spirit allows us to choose life – life in Christ Jesus our Savior.

As you look around at nature this week and begin to see buds on the trees and flowers popping up from the ground, meditate on the goodness of God and the abundant life He brings through our love and obedience to Him, and hold fast to the Creator and guardian of our souls. He truly does bring us from death to life.

NOTES AND REFLECTIONS

April

Fourth Sunday

Contentment in Weakness

Most of us want to be strong. Some exercise to make their bodies stronger. We feel complimented if people view us as mentally and emotionally strong. We like to think we can handle just about anything that comes our way, because we are strong people; however, the Apostle Paul said some perplexing things about his own weaknesses. In II Corinthians 12:10 Paul wrote, "I take pleasure, therefore, in my weakness...for when I am weak, then I am strong." What does this apparent contradiction mean? Just a few verses earlier, Paul explained about his weakness: "And God said, my grace is sufficient for you: for my strength is made perfect in weakness, that the power of Christ may rest upon me" (II Corinthians 12:9). It is when we are weak that God works and we are acutely aware of our total reliance on God. Perhaps we are never as strong as we think we are! It is in weakness, that we give room for God to work though us and make us strong, in His strength.

Recently at church I heard one of my favorite hymns: "It is Well With My Soul." This powerful song was written by a man named Horatio Spafford after two major traumas in his life. The Great Chicago Fire of 1871 ruined him financially after he worked hard to become a wealthy businessman. The second tragedy was much worse. A couple of years after the Chicago Fire, Mr. Spafford lost all four of his daughters when crossing the Atlantic, the ship they were on with their mother, collided with another ship. Spafford's wife Anna survived and sent her husband a telegram which said, "Saved alone." Several weeks later, the ship Spafford was on passed near the spot where his four daughters drowned, and the Holy Spirit, through Spafford's grief and weakness, inspired the words of this great song, "It is Well with My Soul." It truly is in our weakness that God is strong and becomes our strength to enable us to move forward, rather than sink in despair. For those who might be unfamiliar with this song, I will write the first and second verses (there are six verses) to give you an idea of how God can work through great weakness such as grief:

"When peace, like a river, attendeth my way,
When sorrows like sea billows roll;
Whatever my lot, Thou has taught me to say,
It is well, it is well, with my soul.
Though Satan should buffet, though trials should come,
Let this blest assurance control,
That Christ has regarded my helpless estate,
And hath shed His own blood for my soul.
It is well, It is well, with my soul."

God's mighty power is perfected in our weakness. When writing about the trials and sufferings of this life, Paul wrote to the Roman Christians, "the Spirit supports our weaknesses" (Romans 8:26). The writer to the Hebrews also acknowledged our weaknesses, "For we do not have a high priest who is unable to sympathize with our weaknesses..." (Hebrews 4:15). God understands our weaknesses and our need for Him. If you have not yet allowed God to control your life, your weaknesses will eventually surface; it is there we find strength in God who wants to work through us and make us strong. We cannot do it alone.

This week, if a trial, temptation, grief, or disappointment occurs in your life, and you feel weak, or if you know of someone else who is suffering, pray for the contentment of the Apostle Paul or the hymn writer Horatio Spafford. Allow God to work in your life or share God's strength in the life of another, to be made perfect in weakness so that the power of our Lord and Savior can rest upon us.

NOTES AND REFLECTIONS

APRIL

FIFTH SUNDAY

Perseverance

Having no plans for the day, my husband and I got in a Land Rover with our friends in Kenya and drove to Mt. Elgon. We intended to ride around the mountain and view the wild animals (such as the elephants, water buffalo, monkeys and antelopes), and take a short hike through the caves where the elephants sleep at night. Without our knowledge, the guides drove us to the end of the road on the mountain, and told us, "We were going to hike to the top of the mountain and back." After driving for almost an hour, we found out the hike to the top of the mountain and back would take seven exhausting hours.

We did not understand the plan, since everyone was speaking in Swahili, so we did not make preparation for the long hike. We had only one bottle of water between us, and one protein bar to split between five famished people who were also fatigued! During the hike, my husband was asked if he would have chosen to do this, had he known what was entailed, and he simply said, "It's doubtful." However, at the completion of the hike, we were all grateful we did it, and immensely enjoyed the beauty of the mountain.

The hike was similar to our Christian lives and the walk of faith. Often, we are not exactly sure where we are going or what we are supposed to do, but we persevere and continue to hike through the hardships of life. Hebrews 12:1 b-2 a records "Let us run with steadfast endurance, the course that is marked out before us, let this fix your eyes on Jesus the origin and the crown of all faith..." We may become tired and uncertain at times, but like Hebrews Jesus give us the faith needed to persevere.

Growing increasingly tired while on the mountain, this verse in Isaiah came to mind, "But those who wait for the Lord shall renew their strength, they shall mount up with wings like eagles, they shall run and not be weary, they shall walk and not faint" (Isaiah 40:31). The Bible speaks many times of the fatigue, uncertainty and weariness we will surely face in life as believers. Jesus never promised us an easy journey, but He did promise to equip us with all we need to persevere in a world that is not our home. He said in Matthew 11:28, "Come unto Me, all you who are toiling and over-burdened, and I will give you relief."

Challenges and difficulties must be faced along with the unknowns of life, "For we walk by faith, not by vision" (II Corinthians 5:7). We had no idea exactly where the top of the mountain was or how long it would take to get back, but we had a trusted guide to get us there and back safely. Sometimes we have no idea where the Lord is leading; but, again, we must persevere in the faith and trust that He will take us where we need to go, and remain with us, keeping us safe.

The Christian life is one of perseverance, often filled with weariness and uncertainty. Oswald Chambers had a wonderful definition of perseverance that hits the nail on the head: "Perseverance means more than endurance – more than simply holding on until the end. A saint's life is in the hands of God like a bow and arrow in the hands of an archer. God is aiming at something the saint cannot see, but our Lord continues to stretch and strain, and every once in a while the saint says, 'I can't take anymore!' Yet God goes on stretching until His purpose is in sight, and then He lets the arrow fly."

This week, if you grow tied and weary and are uncertain where the Lord is leading, meditate on Chamber's quote and the Scriptures in this devotion, and trust yourself to the Savior, the Good Shepherd, the Lord and our God.

NOTES AND REFLECTIONS

May 2017

Sunday	Monday	Tuesday	Wednesday	Thursday	Friday	Saturday
	1	2	3	4	5	6
7	8	9	10	11	12	13
14	15	16	17	18	19	20
21	22	23	24	25	26	27
28	29	30	31			

May

First Sunday

The Hole

Recorded in a children's folktale is a story of an old woman who found a small hole in her blanket and tried and tried to cut it out until the blanket was all gone. That line from the folktale caused me to think of how life is without Christ, and brought to mind some sections from one of the Wisdom books in the Bible, Ecclesiastes. The author of Ecclesiastes simply called the "Preacher," when contemplating life apart from God wrote, "All is vanity and chasing after the wind" (Ecclesiastes 2:17 b). Like the woman, we often find an empty hole in our lives, and when we try to cut out the hole, we simply create more holes, until at last we find ourselves completely empty and without a covering. Only Christ can completely take out the holes in our lives. It is Jesus who gives life, and gives it abundantly (John 10:10).

In Ecclesiastes 2, the Preacher found an empty spot or hole in his life, and tried to fill it with houses, vineyards, pools, parks and gardens, but the hole became larger. In cutting away at that hole, the Preacher then tried to fill in that hole with male and female slaves, but the hole became even larger. Next he tried to accumulate many possessions: gold, silver, herds and flocks, but the hole once again grew larger. Perhaps singers and many women – concubines, and all "the delights of men" would fill in that space, but the blanket continued to shrink. Finally, the Preacher looked to his wisdom and greatness, and found the blanket was now indeed all gone. He was chasing after the wind, only to come up empty with a life filled with holes and nothingness.

When we look to the world for purpose, happiness, fulfillment, and ultimate joy, we will surely cut away at the fabric of our lives until there is literally nothing left, and "the dust returns to the earth as it was, and the spirit returns to God who gave it" (Ecclesiastes 12:7). Knowing that we will return to God when this life is over, how then are we to live so as not to cut out holes repeatedly until nothing is left? The Preacher said this: "The end of the matter; all has been heard. Fear God and keep His commandments, for this is the whole duty of man" (Ecclesiastes 12:13). Jesus said, in John 14:15, that if we love Him, we will keep His commandments and that by loving God and others, we have kept all of the commandments (Matthew 22:40). Of course we are unable to love God and others perfectly, but when that becomes the focus of our lives, we stop cutting out holes and begin patching them instead with the clothes of righteousness.

NOTES AND REFLECTIONS

MAY

SECOND SUNDAY

Mothers

In the month of May, we celebrate Mother's Day. Jesus esteemed motherhood. In the Gospel of John, chapter 19, while Jesus was suffering and dying on the Cross, He told His closest friend and disciple John to take care of His mother Mary for Him upon His death. In the midst of His horrific suffering, Jesus made provisions for the care of His mother, showing great love and concern for her. "There stood by the cross of Jesus His mother, and His mother's sister, Mary the wife of Cleophas, and Mary Magdalene. When Jesus saw His mother, and the disciple whom He loved standing by, Jesus said to His mother, Woman, behold your son! Then He said to His disciple, Behold, your mother! And from that hour that disciple took her to his home." (John 18:25-27)

After Jesus died and was buried, Mary Magdalene, Mary the mother of James and other women went to the tomb bringing spices to anoint His body, as was the custom in those days. Of course Jesus was no longer there but was resurrected, and to whom did Jesus appear first: a woman, Mary Magdalene. "After Jesus stood up from the grave early on the first day of the week, He appeared first to Mary Magdalene, from whom He had cast out seven demons." (Mark 16:9)

What is the theological significance of His first appearance to a woman? I recall that a cave was a symbol of a womb. In Hebrew, a woman represents a house, specifically her womb, and in Hebrew, a house can also be thought of as a cave. Some believe the manger where Jesus was born was in a cave, as was common in Bethlehem. Jesus was perhaps first born in a cave, and at birth, the first person He would have seen was His mother Mary.

In John 3:16 Jesus told Nicodemus that we must be "born again." Jesus was also "born again" as He rose from the dead, coming out of a cave where He was buried, and then He first saw a woman, Mary Magdalene. In Colossians 1:18, Paul wrote that Jesus was the "first born of the dead", or the "first brought from the grave." Jesus was born of a woman, possibly in a cave, and then appeared first to a woman as He came full circle from His burial cave. We too can come full circle and be born again and be raised with a glorified body, if we believe and trust in Jesus for our salvation.

Throughout Scripture, Jesus showed great love and concern for all mothers, in addition to His own mother. In Luke 7:11-15, Jesus had great compassion on a woman whose only son had died: "And Jesus happened to go out the next day to a city called Nain; and His disciples and a multitude of people went with Him. As He approached the gate of the city He met a funeral procession, the only son of his mother, and she was a widow: and many people of the city were with her. And when the Lord saw her, He had great understanding of her feelings, and said to her, Weep not. And He touched the coffin; and the pallbearers stood still. And he said, Young man, I say to you, Arise. And the corpse sat up and began talking. And Jesus delivered him to his mother." Jesus truly understood the love of a mother.

This month as we celebrate Mother's Day or think about mother-hood, remember how important mothers were to Jesus. For those whose mother has already left this earth, or who have had challenging relationships with their mothers, pause for a moment and simply give thanks to God for the wonderful gift of life, that comes through our mothers. (Credit given to Joshua Collins for much of his theological insight in this devotion.)

NOTES AND REFLECTIONS

MAY

THIRD SUNDAY

The Forest and the Trees

A man who occasionally eats lunch at the Mission, often calls me over to ask some biblical questions, and tries to engage me in arguments and debates about the Christian faith. While I am open to talking about the Faith, I generally try to avoid arguments. This man appears rather knowledgeable and is interesting, but he sometimes gets upset when I merely listen without debate. Recently at lunch, he waved, called me over as usual, but then said something delightful. "You know, I've had an epiphany! As you know I'm a doubting Thomas and I don't know if I believe that Jesus even actually existed, but as I was thinking about various religions and the supposed words of Jesus, I now see it's simply all about love – just love." I smiled, knowing I had nothing to do with his epiphany, and said, "Sometimes we can't see the forest for the trees" and then we both laughed. I said, "Keep thinking about that as you explore the Christian faith, and remember the greatest commandments in the Bible – love God and love your neighbor as yourself; even Jesus said love sums up the whole Law. It is truly all about love." (Matthew 22:37-40, Mark 12:29-31 and Luke 10:25-28).

At a recent Mission staff meeting we read Romans 12:9, "Let love be without hypocrisy" and also the "love chapter," I Corinthians 13 which declares that love is the greatest of all things, and even if we do "great" and "holy" things, like preaching and teaching, exercising spiritual gifts, developing a strong faith, giving all we have to the poor, even giving up our very lives, if we do not have love, the Apostle Paul said we have nothing. Mother Teresa once said, "We can do no great things, only small things with great love." Is that not what I Corinthians 13 teaches? We can know Scripture backward and forward, in Greek and Hebrew, we can preach and teach, we can take difficult mission trips, we can do many pious and wonderful things, but if we do them for the wrong reason or with a wrong motive, and if we do anything without love, we have accomplished nothing.

Mother Teresa also said, "Intense love does not measure, it just gives," and again, "Give until it hurts with a smile." Apart from Christ, we can never truly and fully love, expecting nothing in return, and still simply love. As human beings with a fallen sinful nature, we generally love those who love us; we love people who are easy to love, and people who do kind things for us. At times, we may keep tabs to make sure we don't give more than we receive; but Jesus calls us to love as He loves – without measure, to love the unlovable, and to love even our enemies (Matthew 5:44).

Others may want to engage us in theological discussions (which may be beneficial), and they may want to ask all kinds of questions, but what people will notice most is our love for them, even if they act unlovable. People need to see Jesus in us, and if we are Christ followers, we must obey the two greatest Bible commandments - to love God with all we have, and to love our neighbor as ourselves. This week, ask Jesus to give us that love that we cannot have apart from Him, so that others may find Christ through God's love. Review these words from Mother Teresa.

WISDOM FROM MOTHER TERESA

People are often unreasonable and self-centered.

Forgive them anyway.

If you are kind, people may accuse you of ulterior motives.

Be kind anyway.

If you are honest, people may cheat you.

Be honest anyway.

If you find happiness, people may be jealous.

Be happy anyway.

The Good you do today may be forgotten tomorrow.

Do good anyway.

Give the world the best you have and it may never be enough.

Give your best anyway.

For you see, in the end, it is between you and God.

It was never between you and them anyway.

–Mother Teresa

NOTES AND REFLECTIONS

MAY

FOURTH SUNDAY

Ministry Life

A question was asked during staff meeting, "Is ministry easy?" The answer – "No, ministry is not easy!" Today, my plans were to remain in my office for an hour or so, reading my Bible and writing my weekly devotion, but that did not happen. "Ministry" got in the way. Clients came to the Mission and stayed late. Some were confused, others were upset, a few were homeless, and most came with a multitude of problems that could not even be imagined. In the back of my mind was the feeling, "There is no time for this; I need to write my devotional!"

I realized my thinking was wrong, I was where the need was and people needed my ministry more than the staff needed a devotional. Why? "I was called to listen to the needs of others, even those unspoken." We must listen to others, even if the conversation does not make sense, and even if there were nothing we could do to solve their problems. Prayer is the heart of ministry. When the answer is beyond our hands, the old adage rings true, "Prayer changes people and people changes things!"

The gospels record where Jesus attempted to go to a quiet place to be alone, but the crowds followed Him, and He still ministered to their needs, whatever they were. When Jesus heard about the death of his friend and cousin John the Baptist, He mourned John's death and wanted time alone, but the crowds once again followed Him. Scripture recorded that Jesus "had compassion on them" (Matthew 14:14) and cured the sick and tended to the people's needs. Jesus was often tired, even to the point of sleeping in a boat through a terrible storm (Matthew 8)!

Ministry is hard work, and not always on the daily schedule. Ministry often interrupts plans. This is not to advocate poor self-care, no rest or family time, and no boundaries, but sometimes ministry truly does seem to get in the way of things we want to do. Also, there may not always be time to do other "ministries" we wanted to do. I am learning, slowly, to think that maybe once in a while (or more often than not!) that is o.k. God's plans are often different than ours, and He brings challenging people to us who take our time and energy...but isn't that what ministry is all about? Giving ourselves freely to others!

Today there is little time to write a weekly devotion, but it will not be a planned one. The planned one would have taken more time and biblical research than was available. Today it was a simple devotion of realizing my humanness, my limitations, my incorrect motives and attitudes, my impatience, and my weak attempt to flow where God leads. But what is truly amazing, is that God still leads me even though my following may be a bit begrudgingly! What a gracious God we serve.

NOTES AND REFLECTIONS

June 2017

Sunday	Monday	Tuesday	Wednesday	Thursday	Friday	Saturday
				1	2	3
4	5	6	7	8	9	10
11	12	13	14	15	16	17
18	19	20	21	22	23	24
25	26	27	28	29	30	

JUNE

FIRST SUNDAY

The Problem of Faith

Hebrews chapter 11 is considered a "Hall of Faith." This chapter recounts the great people of faith throughout sacred history and what they accomplished, by the grace of God, through their faith. The chapter begins, "Now faith is the reality of things being hoped for, the proof of things not seen" (Hebrews 11:1). What this particular chapter does not always mention though, are the great difficulties many of these people endured as they lived out their faith.

For example, Noah is mentioned for building the Ark to save his family, but what is not mentioned is the ridicule that he endured from those around him as he built the Ark. We also read about the great faith of Abraham. God told Abraham to leave his home and family and go to a foreign land that he knew nothing about. Abraham was then called to sacrifice his only son, Isaac, though fortunately God stopped him in the midst of this test. Imagine though the anguish Abraham must have felt during this trial. Joseph is also mentioned and Hebrews does not mention the fact that this great man of faith was sold by his brothers, was falsely imprisoned, and suffered many years before God elevated him in Egypt. Moses is mentioned, who struggled to lead thousands of belligerent, complaining people for forty years through the wilderness toward the Promise Land.

Many are mentioned in Hebrews 11, who suffered ridicule, stoning, imprisonment, some were sawed in two, killed with the sword, others were forced to hide in caves or holes in the ground, some wandered through deserts and rough mountain terrain, and all lived difficult lives. Scripture declared that these people were all commended for their faith, yet many did not live to see the promises of God for their faithful obedience.

The life of faith and obedience is never easy. God never promised an easy journey to the Kingdom, but He did promise His peace and that He would always be with us. Some question why faithful followers of Jesus suffered so much or faced such trials and difficulties in life. I do not have an answer, but look at Hebrews chapter 11 and see that all great people of faith, who God used in extraordinary ways, also lived trying lives. God told the Apostle Paul that He "will show him the great things he must suffer for My name's sake" (Acts 9:16). The hope and assurance though that we can live with through our trials, is that as we are being refined by fire like gold, we are strengthened, and we are made ready for God's eternal Kingdom where we will live in glory forever. One thing is certain, "The end is worth the journey!"

NOTES AND REFLECTIONS

JUNE

SECOND SUNDAY

Our View of God

How do we react, when difficult things happen in life? Well, that may depend on the circumstances or the exact nature of the difficulty, right? To a certain degree, yes, but in all cases, we need to turn to God and hold onto our faith, believing He is always a good God. We might ask, "Why is God allowing this pain, this trial, this difficulty into my life in the first place? What is He doing with it? What can I learn from this situation?" Perhaps most importantly, "How will I respond to God in the midst of pain and difficulty?" The answers to all questions depend mostly on who God is and what we know in faith to be His attributes.

Is God the loving Heavenly Father who wants only good things for us? How do we define "good" things? The gospel explained, "If you, being human, provide good gifts for your children: how much more will your heavenly Father give the gift of the Holy Spirit to those who ask Him?" (Luke 11:13). First of all, what does God think is the most important gift we can receive? Himself – the Comforter, the Paraclete, the Holy Spirit. Why? Of all the gifts God wants to give us the best gifts, which include most importantly, Himself, in the Holy Spirit. The Holy Spirit gives us wisdom, comfort, strength, power, all the things needed to get through this life – especially when life becomes difficult.

Scripture promises to supply our earthly needs, in addition to the spiritual need for the guidance of the Holy Spirit. Jesus said, as recorded in the gospels, that we need not worry about the things of life such as food, clothing, etc., but that, "Your Father knows you need these things, but rather seek first the kingdom of God and all these things shall be added to you" (Luke 12:30-31).

In other words, God loves us and will provide for us, but His primary goal is for us to seek Him, to seek the kingdom of God, and to desire His Holy Spirit; after that, He will provide for our needs. Do we really believe this? Do we really believe God is only good and loving towards His children? An old pastor friend once wrote me a brief note many years ago, when my life was very difficult, and the note I have kept to this day. He wrote, "Life is like a grindstone, and whether it grinds you down or polishes you, depends on the stuff you are made of. It also depends on your view of God." How do you view God? The Bible declares that all God does and allows is for His glory and for our good. The big question is "Is life grinding you down or polishing you?"

NOTES AND REFLECTIONS

JUNE

THIRD SUNDAY

Our Good Father

In June we celebrate Father's Day. Some people celebrate and enjoy Father's Day, while for others it may be a painful day with perhaps no celebrations. There are people who never knew their birth fathers, or their father has passed on, or their father has abandoned them, or who had bad relationships with their fathers. For those who live with the pain of a distant or unknown father, I am truly sorry for your hurt. Fortunately, no matter what our earthly fathers are or were, we have a wonderful heavenly Father who loves us unconditionally and promised never to leave or forsake us (Hebrews 13:5).

I have heard arguments as to why Jesus came as a man, rather than as a woman. I have heard questions why we refer to God as our Father (as Jesus did) and not as our mother. Father Simon, a Priest friend from Chicago, once told me something interesting concerning these gender questions, which makes it an honor to refer to God as our Father. In ancient days, when a child was born, everyone of course knew who the mother was, but the identity of the father may come into question and doubt. For God to call Himself our Father, He is saying there is no doubt to whom we belong, and He proudly acknowledges His children and willingly and delightfully cares for them.

In the ancient Near East, a King would refer to his subjects as "children," and to himself as their "father." God, our King, also repeatedly referred to the people of Israel, especially Solomon, as His children, and called Himself their Father (1 Chronicles 17:13, 22:10, 28:6). Jesus also refers to us as His children throughout Scripture, and called God our Father.

In the Sermon on the Mount, (Matthew 6 and Luke 12), Jesus spoke of God as a generous, caring and loving Father, who promised to provide all that we need. Jesus said, "Stop worrying about your life, what you will eat; neither about clothes...your Father knows that you need these things, but rather seek the kingdom of God and all these things shall be added to you; for it is your Father's good pleasure to give you the kingdom " (Luke 12:22, 30 b, 31, 32 b). Our Heavenly Father truly wants to give us many good things, including the best – His self and His eternal Kingdom.

If it is difficult for you to celebrate Father's Day, remember that God is your Father and is an Abba Father to all. Jesus called to God, the Father on the Cross, "Father, forgive them for they know not what they do." The Apostle Paul wrote, "The Holy Spirit joins with our human spirit confirming that we are the children of God" (Romans 8:16). This week, and always, celebrate your relationship to the Heavenly Father!

NOTES AND REFLECTIONS

JUNE

FOURTH SUNDAY

A Memorable Legacy

Recently during morning coffee and Bible reading, my husband decided to pull an old Bible off the shelf, instead of the one he had been reading. The Bible he chose belonged to my father, who lived in a house I owned for a year with his wife until his death. I had given my dad this Bible for his 67th birthday, and I was delighted to see it was tattered, worn, written in, and obviously read often. On the front cover were a few verses dad had written. I was interested to discover which verses had been important to him; however, what was written underneath the passages was what intrigued me and deeply touched my heart. Dad had written, "See you in heaven. Love, Dad." I wondered if he wrote that near the end of his life when he was under hospice care, or exactly when he wrote those precious words.

My dad had a strong faith and was a long-time Gideon, which was an important part of his life. Dad loved his Saturday morning breakfast meetings with the Gideon brothers, and he loved distributing Bibles. He was active in his church, involved with prison ministries, and by the looks of his old Bible he read it far more frequently than most do. Two of the verses dad had written on his Bible were Psalm 41:3, "The Lord sustains them on their sickbed; in their illness you heal all their infirmities," and James 5:16,

"Acknowledge your failures and side steps one to another, and pray for yourselves and for one another, that you may be made spiritually whole again. When a righteous man prays fervently there is great power in prayer."

The previous verses in James 5 dealt with calling the elders of the church to pray for restoration in sickness, but dad did not write those down, nor do I remember him asking for physical healing. What I do remember is on one visit of the pastor when dad was in a hospital bed under hospice care, dad told him, "You know, I've always believed in eternal life, and now that I know I'm getting close, I'm kind of anxious!" Dad had a great peace about his approaching death because of his strong faith.

When I shared with my siblings what we found written in dad's Bible, one of my sisters said, "Dad was a good example of how life should end - with a good attitude." What a wonderful legacy to leave to his family. Dad's words written in his Bible were words that he obviously wanted us to see after he was gone. This brought thoughts of the legacy that all leave loved ones. Do we have the attitude that Christ wants us to have, even in the face of death? What do others see as we profess Christ? Will I have the strength that my dad had as he approached his mortality? Is my faith that strong?

As a former hospice chaplain, I have seen many people face death and a common thought in hospice is that we die in the same manner that we live. How do we live, and is our faith evident to others? Do we live with the assurance of a good God who never leaves or forsakes us, up until the end of life? I am grateful for a wonderful Christian father and hope not only to end my life in the peaceful manner, but to also live each day with the same strong faith.

NOTES AND REFLECTIONS

July 2017

Sunday	Monday	Tuesday	Wednesday	Thursday	Friday	Saturday
						1
2	3	4	5	6	7	8
9	10	11	12	13	14	15
16	17	18	19	20	21	22
23 30	24 31	25	26	27	28	29

July

First Sunday

Freedom in Christ

As we celebrate America's history and the freedoms and privileges of democracy, we as Christians should also remember the freedom we have in Christ. Human nature longs for freedom, which God placed within us all. People around the world have an innate desire for freedom. Countries, including our own, have fought hard for freedom and many have given their lives for this freedom. The Bible often speaks of freedom and we truly do have freedom when we have Christ. "Christ freed us, therefore continue to stand firm for this freedom, and stop allowing yourself to be entangled in a yoke of slavery." (Galatians 5:1). From what did Christ free us? He freed us from guilt, from death, from condemnation, from the burden of sin, from the cares of this world, and gave us freedom through the shed blood of Jesus.

To live according to God's Word and His precepts is not living under a heavy burden, but is actually living in total and complete freedom. "I will walk about in freedom for I have sought out your precepts." (Psalm 119:45). Scripture declares that if we love God and our neighbor, we have obeyed all of the laws (Mark 12:30). However, Psalm 119:32 recorded, "I run in the path of your commands, for you have set my heart free." In II Corinthians 3:17 Paul wrote, "Now the Lord is that Spirit: and where the Spirit of the Lord is there is freedom." James wrote that the "perfect law," God's law of love, gives us freedom.

Back in the Garden of Eden, God told Adam and Eve they were free to eat of any fruit in the garden, but not of the Tree of the Knowledge of Good and Evil, or they would die (Genesis 2:16). Adam and Eve abused their freedom, and not only they, but all of humankind now dies. God gives us freedom, but commands us to never abuse that freedom. The Apostle Paul wrote to the church in Galatia about the potential abuse of freedom when, "Brethren, God called you to freedom; but do not make your freedom an excuse for a corrupt nature, but by love serve one another. For the whole law is fulfilled in one word, even love; you shall love your neighbor as yourself" (Galatians 5:13-14).

When Jesus began His ministry, He spoke in the Temple and quoted from the scroll of Isaiah 61. "The Spirit of the Lord is upon me, and has consecrated me to tell glad tidings to the destitute; and sent me to proclaim deliverance (freedom) to the captives, and recovery of sight to the blind, and to set at liberty (freedom) the downtrodden..." (Luke 4:18).

When we live in God's Truth, we live in freedom. Jesus said, "If you continue in My word, then you are without a doubt My disciples; and you will know the truth, and the truth will make you free" (John 8:31-32). This week as we celebrate National Independence and our freedoms in this country, remember the ultimate freedom we have in Christ, and in love, live within the Truth of that freedom.

NOTES AND REFLECTIONS

July

Second Sunday

God on My Mind

Romans 12:12 instructs believers to, "be persistent in the habit of prayer" or to "persevere in prayer" or to be "faithful" or "constant in prayer," depending on which translation you read. Persistence in prayer is a life-style of continuous turning to God in all things and in all circumstances, always thinking of God first and praying to Him.

In a recent staff meeting, Jim spoke about a car accident. The man in the accident said as the car was swerving out of control, all he could think to do was to cry out to God for help. In frightening and difficult times, it may be easier to call out to God than in good times, but I humbly admit, sometimes even a seasoned Christian such as myself is not always "persistent in the habit of prayer" and does not always call out to God first before asking others for help.

Traveling in Kenya as a short-term missionary, Alan, a young friend was driving, and his mom was in the back seat. I was in the passenger seat of a large four door pick-up truck. We finally came to a smooth road (which is rare in East Africa), and since there are almost no stop lights or stop signs in Kenya, Alan was able to pick up speed and we were driving about 50 miles per hour. Suddenly out of nowhere, two small children ran across the street right in front of the truck! Since most people in Kenya do not have cars, many walked on both sides of the road. All of a sudden, every-thing went into slow motion. With a young driver, without a lot of driving experience, the question was, "How does the driver avoid hitting the children?" I simply looked over at him, speechless, thinking I was going to die or be so mangled that I wished I were dead. I watched the ground quickly approach our windshield as we went flying into a ditch.

My thoughts turned to Alan's driving and myself. I was not praying without ceasing. I was just thinking how, or if we would get through this accident. Alan remained silent. Fortunately, from the back seat his mother was, "persistent in the habit of prayer," and simply shouted, "Jesus, Jesus, Jesus!" The truck came to a sudden stop as we slammed into a ditch at high speed. Turned on our side, we managed to get out of the truck to see if we hit anyone – especially the two small children. I had fallen onto Alan, but we were both o.k. (we were not wearing our seat belts!) We managed to crawl out of the truck, all unhurt, miraculously no one on the road was hit, and even the truck did not have any damage. To my amazement, a group of men who were walking along the road and witnessed what had just happened came and picked up the truck, turned it up right and put it back on the road, and off we went!

I humbly admit, and I pray each day, that many of you reading this would learn to be persistent, constant, and faithful in prayer. Isn't it amazing that even though we did not turn immediately to God in that Kenya accident, our loving and merciful Lord still protected all of us from harm? "If we are faithless, He remains faithful - for he cannot deny Himself." (II Timothy 2:13). Thank God for His constant faithfulness!

NOTES AND REFLECTIONS

JULY
THIRD SUNDAY

Second Chances

Working at the Rescue Mission, we all meet people who really love the Lord and who desire to be Christ-followers, but some of our clients often struggle with various strongholds, temptations, addictions, and weaknesses. They repent, vow not to fall into sin again, but eventually, sometimes sooner than later, fall again. Perhaps some of you can relate to this struggle as well. What does the Bible teach concerning our sinful nature, our weaknesses and our struggles with sin?

Some of the greatest men in the Bible struggled with sinful behavior. Remember when Jesus' strong and faithful disciple Peter said he would be willing to die for his Savior Jesus, yet three times – not once - but three times he denied even knowing Jesus? "And Jesus said, all of you will stumble and be tempted to sin: for it is written, I will fatally strike down the Shepherd, and the sheep will be scattered. But Peter said, Even though, all shall be scattered from you, yet I will not stumble." (Mark 14:27, 29, 30). Yet Mark 14, Matthew 27 and John 18 all recount Peter's denial of Jesus after He was arrested; however, Peter was full of remorse for this sin and Scripture says he "sobbed" after he denied knowing Jesus. How did Jesus react to Peter's sin? In John 21:15-17, Jesus asked Peter three times if he loved Him, since three times Peter denied Him. Jesus still loved and forgave Peter, and gave him not just one chance to get it right, but three chances.

Paul spoke of his intense struggles with sin when he wrote, "For what I do I do not tolerate: for what I would do, I do not do: but what I detest, that I do. Now it is no more I who does wrong, but sin that dwells in me. For I know there is nothing good in my earthly nature: for the desire to do right is there, but I cannot find the power to do the good things. For the good things I want to do, I do not: but I do the wrong things that I do not want to do. Now if I do what I do not want to do, it is no more me doing the wrong, but sin that resides in me... At heart I consent gladly to the law of God as far as my new nature is concerned: but I see another principle working in my body, warring against the law of my mind, and bringing me into bondage to the law of sin which operates in my human nature. I am an unacceptable man! Who shall deliver me from the body of death? I thank God for deliverance through Christ Jesus our Lord (Romans 7:15-20, 22-25).

While God is full of mercy and compassion, and He always forgives when we repent and turn back to Him, He does command us though to, "go and sin no more" as He told the women caught in adultery who was about to be stoned (John 8:11) and offers deliverance, as Paul stated above.

We were born into sin and live with a sinful nature; so like many of our clients, we too will continue to struggle through this earthly life. However, we do have the power of the Holy Spirit, who allows us to live in His power and to resist temptation. Paul wrote, "No test has come your way but such as is common to man: God is faithful, who will not permit you to be tempted beyond your endurance; but will with each test also show you a way of escape, so that you will be victorious" (I Corinthians 10:13). When we stop trying to live on our own, but rather become bond servants of the Lord Jesus, He can, and will, give us victory in this broken world.

While it is not our job to judge the world, but God's, it is our job to share in love and compassion the hope and the victory that comes through the power of the Holy Spirit with those we meet, and to share the abundant life Jesus promised all those who come to him. Let us walk besides those who struggle, hold them up in love, and share God's love, mercy and grace as we journey to the Kingdom together. As the book of Ecclesiastes recorded "Two are better than one, because they have a good reward for their toil. For if they fall, one will lift up the other; but woe to one who is alone and falls and does not have another to help. Though one may be overpowered by another, two can withstand him. And a threefold cord is not easily broken" (Ecclesiastes 4:9-10, 12).

NOTES AND REFLECTIONS

JULY

FOURTH SUNDAY

The White Stone

There is a precious white stone spoken of in Revelation, "To everyone who conquers I will give some of the hidden manna, and I will give a white stone, and on the white stone is written a new name that no one knows except the one who receives it." (Revelation 2:17). What is the significance of a white stone?

In ancient times during a court trial, when the person charged with a crime was heard and the evidence given for and against that person, the jury would pass around a wooden box for the verdict. If a juror thought the person was guilty, they would place a black stone in the box, but if they thought the person was not guilty, they would place a white stone in the box. When each person placed their stone in the box, the judge would count the white stones and the black stones to pronounce the final verdict. If more white stones than black stones were in the box, the person would be found not guilty, pardoned, and given their freedom. As proof of their pardon, the King would imprint his name on the white stone. They would carry their white stone with them in case anyone who knew they had been to court asked for their proof of pardon.

What a beautiful picture we have of the King of Glory giving us a white stone, pronouncing us fully pardoned, forgiven, with the freedom to live with Him forever in eternity. All our past sins are gone. "Who can lay any charge upon God's chosen ones? It is God who gives right standing with Him." (Romans 8:33). All of our boxes should be filled with nothing but black stones, yet Christ has taken them for us, put them in His box, took on our penalty, then replaced the black stones with all white stones, making us holy and blameless before Him.

NOTES AND REFLECTIONS

JULY
FIFTH SUNDAY

A Radical Love

"The Love Chapter" is found in I Corinthians 13, written by the Apostle Paul. This chapter is often read at weddings because it describes the ultimate, perfect, and complete form of love. It describes the love that God has for us, and a love God calls us to share in, but a love that when reading this passage carefully, we can unfortunately never quite emulate. However, we are indeed called to love in this manner. Let's take a hard look, line by line, at exactly what Paul wrote:

"Love is long-suffering and sympathetic," or in other translations love is "patient and kind." Do we love, and also show love, when someone is insulting us, hurting us, getting on our nerves or annoying us? Do we love freely when others are unkind to us? How long-suffering are we really?! "Love has no jealousy." Have you ever found yourself maybe not jealous of another person, but jealous of someone's time or their heart? Have you ever been jealous of something someone else has, or someone else's position in life? If we have been, do we still truly love that person?

"Love is not anxious to impress others, does not hold inflated ideas of self-importance." In other translations love "does not envy or boast." Have you ever felt the need to prove yourself, or perhaps "show off" to others in regards to your talents, your education, your achievements, your knowledge, your finances or whatever? Love "has good manners" in other translations love "is not rude." Have you ever acted rudely, said something rude or disrespectful in anger, even to people you love, and perhaps to the people you love most?

Love is not "self-seeking." Have you ever thought, even for a second, "What's in it for me?" How can this person benefit me? Have you ever thought, how can this person make ME happy, instead of focusing on how can I make this other person happy, even if it does not make me happy? Love is "never provoked," and "does not keep score of wrongs." Other translations write, love "is not irritable or resentful." When someone has hurt us deeply, do we hold that against them? Do we ever remind them of that pain they caused us? Are we holding on to the poison of unforgiveness (Matthew 18: 21-35) or bitterness? Love, "takes no pleasure in wrongdoing, but rejoices when truth is victorious." Have you ever felt pleasure in being right and proving another wrong? Verse seven says, "There is no limit to endurance, love has endless faith and great expectations, there is no end to love's tolerance." Many people know verse seven from other translations as, "Love bears all things, believes all things, hopes all things, endures all things." Notice the word "all" in this sentence. All, means, well, ALL! Do we have limits to our love? Do we endure all things in love? And finally verse eight, "Love stands when all else disintegrates" or "Love never ends." Like the marriage vows of loving for better or worse, whatever that may entail, does our love still stand, as we may watch everything around us disintegrate? (1 Corinthians 13:4-8).

Next time you read I Corinthians 13, the Love Chapter, instead of reading it quickly and marveling at how beautiful it sounds, reflect on the difficulty of loving in that manner, but also the beauty of that kind of love. Pray that our loving God will enable our hearts and minds to love as this chapter teaches us to love.

NOTES AND REFLECTIONS

August 2017

Sunday	Monday	Tuesday	Wednesday	Thursday	Friday	Saturday
		1	2	3	4	5
6	7	8	9	10	11	12
13	14	15	16	17	18	19
20	21	22	23	24	25	26
27	28	29	30	31		

AUGUST

FIRST SUNDAY

Servanthood

All of us have done things we really do not want to do, but perhaps felt an obligation or did not know how to say, "No," but then we also often complain, even though we know we did the right thing and did what needed to be done. 1 Peter 4:9-10 "Never begrudge the hospitality to one another. As each has received a gift from God, so let all use such gifts in the service of one another, as good stewards of God's multi-sided grace." What gifts do we each have that we can share with others? Do we have extra time, talents/ skills, or maybe a surplus of money? God gives us these things in order for us to share them and to be hospitable with one another, not to keep them to ourselves or live our lives only to please ourselves.

Perhaps one of the most difficult aspects of the Christian life is to realize fully that we are not our own. In Romans 1:1 and Titus 1:1 the Apostle Paul called himself a "bondservant of Jesus Christ." In Philippians 1:1, both Paul and Timothy called themselves "bondservants of Jesus Christ." The disciple James said he was "subject to God" in his letter to the Jews (James 1:1), and Peter said he was "a servant and an apostle of Jesus Christ" (2 Peter 1:1). James' brother Jude also said he was a "servant of Jesus Christ" (Jude 1:1).

What does it mean to be a servant or a bondservant? Servants are unable to do their own will, but can only do what their master tells them. If God is our Master, as well as Lord and Savior, then we are His bondservants and must give up our own rights; we can only do what He tells us. So why do we fight that so much? Why does our sinful human nature keep getting in the way? We truly are not our own, but we have been bought with a price – a large price – the very life of Jesus.

When we become Christ – followers, we give up our rights and are "subject to God" to do His will. When God calls us to use that which He has given us in service to others, we are to obey His command as our Master, and without complaint!

Like maybe some of you, I struggle in this area. How often do we do something for someone, and then complain about it? How often do we want our time to be for ourselves, rather than in service to others? How much of our days do we want for our own plans and pleasures, neglecting other more important duties or people? We are not our own, but were bought with a price (1 Corinthians 6:19-20), bought and kept close in love by our Master. Our time is not our own. Our money is not our own. Our talents, skills and knowledge are not our own. Our bodies are not our own. We are not our own, but everything about us, belongs to our Master and Maker – God.

NOTES AND REFLECTIONS

AUGUST

SECOND SUNDAY

God, Self, and Others

Chaplains go through a year of special training called Clinical Pastoral Education (CPE). One component of CPE often focuses on what our relationship is to God, self, and others. These three relationships are important for the chaplain to think about concerning his or her ministry. For all of us who serve Christ, in whatever capacity He has called us, either professionally or as lay people, how do these relationships to God, self and others affect our own life, relationships, and work? How do our faith struggles, self-doubts, or our challenging relationships affect what we do and say as we live as Christ followers?

I think of Moses in Exodus 4:10 when he told God that basically he was unable to lead the people of Israel because he was "slow of speech" and they would not listen to him, even though God had previously told Moses that the people "will listen to your voice" (Exodus 3:18). Like many of us, perhaps Moses focused on his own limitations and weaknesses, and not only felt unsure of himself, but perhaps also struggled with believing that God could indeed use him as He said. If in our relationship with God we doubt that He can use us, we also struggle with self-doubt, or our relationship with self. These doubts will then affect our relationship with others to whom we should serve, and also our faith in God who said He will equip us. Moses struggled with his relationship perhaps with self, which in turn caused him to doubt what greatness God would do through him, which would have ultimately affected his relationship with the people of Israel had he not followed through on God's call for his life.

Paul apparently was not an eloquent speaker either; "Although I may be unskilled in speaking, I am not in knowledge" (II Corinthians 11:6). In all of II Corinthians 11, Paul felt the need to defend himself and his ministry against his critics, yet he maintained that he would continue with his ministry because of his love for God and even his love for his critics. Fortunately though, Paul knew the writings of Moses, and knew how God used Moses in such a mighty way, even when Moses was unsure of himself.

Like Moses, Paul spoke about the struggles that occurred in his life of ministry, He wrote, "I take pleasure, therefore, in my weakness, ill-treatment, necessary hardships, troubles and difficulties, when they are distresses for Christ's sake: for when I am weak, then I am strong" (II Corinthians 12:10). Paul also struggled with his "thorn in the flesh" that God would not take away, even though Paul pleaded for God to do so (II Corinthians 12:7-8). God used Paul to spread the Gospel to many nations of the world and to start many churches, despite his personal weaknesses. God uses a humble spirit to do His mighty work, as He did with both Moses and Paul, despite their personal limitations.

When we have self-doubts like Moses, thinking God could not possibly use us, or when we experience challenges and "thorns in the flesh" like Paul, we can consider what their relationships were with God, self, and others, that made them effective and powerful men of God. Moses' and Paul's relationship to God was faith, their relationship with self was humility, and their relationship with others, was love and a desire for others to know the power and grace of Christ.

This week, think about what your relationships are with God, self, and others. Ask Him to give you faith, humility, and a heart of love as you allow God to work through the weak vessels in which we all live.

NOTES AND REFLECTIONS

AUGUST

THIRD SUNDAY

Multi-Culturalism

The Christian faith is a faith that embraces people from all walks of life, and should intentionally reach out to people of all races, cultures and classes. The Apostle Paul, a very educated Jewish man, had a ministry amongst the Gentiles, or non-Jews, of whom he had to learn to relate. Many scholars think Paul was very specific in speaking the language of the various people he ministered to in II Corinthians 4:5, 6 where he wrote, "For we preach not ourselves, but Christ Jesus the Lord; and ourselves your servants for Jesus' sake. The same God who caused light" (Jewish thought) "to shine out of darkness' has caused His light to shine within our hearts, to give the light of understanding" (Greek thought) "of the glory" (Roman thought) "of God in the face of Jesus Christ."

Paul knew specifically what words to use to pique the interests of various types of people in order to share Christ. Our work and ministry is never about us, but only about Christ's light, knowledge, and glory as we serve Him as slaves and bondservants to all people. Paul also said in I Corinthians 9:19, 22, "For though I am free from the authority of all men, yet I have made myself servant to all, that I might win more converts... To the weak I became weak, that I might win the weak: I am made all things to all men that I might by all means save some."

The apostle Paul recognized the multi-cultural aspect of the Christian message and that it does not belong to any one people group or culture. Paul wrote, "For we are all the children of God by faith in Christ Jesus. For as many as have been identified with Christ by baptism have been clothed with the attributes of Christ. In Christ there is neither Jew nor Greek, bond nor free, male nor female; for you are all one in Christ Jesus. And if you belong to Christ, then you are Abraham's offspring and Abraham's promise is your promise" (Galatians 3:26-29). The faith that Christ preached quickly spread throughout the whole world, and it is a faith given for all people. God desires all people, from all nations, to come to Him. 2 Peter 3:9 says, "The Lord is not slow concerning His promise as some count slowness; but is long suffering to all, not wishing any to perish, but desiring all to take the way of repentance."

Missionaries are acutely aware of the multi-cultural facet of the Christian faith and have learned how to share the Good News of Jesus Christ in culturally appropriate ways. Hebrews 13:8 records, "Jesus Christ is the same yesterday, and today, and forever," but Jesus is perceived differently from culture to culture. Our various sociological conditionings (such as our race, gender, economic status, politics, education etc.), all influence our view of Christ. However, trying to understand and respect those differences, and, "becoming all things to all people" as the apostle Paul did, will enable others to see through their own culture, and to know the love and grace of our Savior Jesus Christ.

As we share our faith in an ever increasing multi-cultural society, may we have the mind and heart of Paul as we seek to win as many as possible to Christ. May we pray this week for Christ to help us love all people and to share the Good News with all of those to whom God places in our path each day.

NOTES AND REFLECTIONS

AUGUST

FOURTH SUNDAY

Horses and Chariots

My husband recently bought a much needed car. Two days later, the car would not start; it was completely dead. At this point, he was not at all happy. In his disappointment, he asked me if I had a Bible verse that might make him feel better about the situation. Since he said his "chariot" was not running. I immediately thought of Psalm 20:7-8 where King David wrote, "Some take pride in chariots, and some in horses, but our pride (or "trust" in other versions) is in the name of the Lord our God. They will collapse and fall, but we shall rise and stand upright." He was delighted that I came up with such verses. He did indeed find comfort in those words, which he then quickly looked up to read for himself. Paul was a relatively new Christian, and was surprised that there were verses in the Bible for almost everything in life. In reality though, we should always meditate on Scripture, no matter what is going on in our lives. "All Scripture is inspired by God and is useful for teaching, for reproof, for correction, and for training in righteousness, so that everyone who belongs to God may be proficient, equipped for every good work" (II Timothy 3:16 NRSV).

In this life we can often be disappointed in things, in situations, even in people. Life does not always go our way, and there are always bumps in the road. Some have heard the saying, "We are either in a storm, coming out of a storm, or about to go through a storm." The storms of life can be rough and dangerous, or they can simply be inconvenient. No matter what the storm, there is indeed Scripture that can guide and comfort us.

In the front of many Bibles, and in all Gideon distributed Bibles, there is a section that shows where portions of Scripture can be found when we are in the midst of trouble, or sadness, or worries, when we need comfort, or freedom from fears, doubts, etc. since the Bible does indeed address every area of human life. We should become familiar with the Bible so when someone does ask us a biblical question, or has a need, or confronts us in our faith, we can humbly go to God's Word and give an answer. Peter wrote, "If anyone asks you to give an account of the hope which you cherish, be ready at all times to answer with a teachable spirit and a wonder that is inspired by a sacred trust" (I Peter 3:15).

This is a "hurry, worry" world, but, as Christians we need to set aside time each day to read God's Word and learn more about the God we serve and the faith we profess. The Bible is the place where God speaks to us, where He reveals Himself to us, and where we are instructed in how to live the Christian life. After all, if we are staking our lives and our eternities on the words of Scripture, it is a wise thing to know the Scripture. There are many commentaries and study guides to assist in understanding the Bible, and there are readable and easy to understand translations. People throughout the world have risked their lives and even died for reading the Bible, and in this country we have complete freedom to know God better through His Holy Word.

     This week, try to set aside a time each day to review the devotions and read your Bible. Ask the Holy Spirit to help you understand and listen as God quietly speaks to your heart. Remember, your <u>hEARt</u> has a spiritual ear! Listen!

NOTES AND REFLECTIONS

September 2017

Sunday	Monday	Tuesday	Wednesday	Thursday	Friday	Saturday
					1	2
3	4	5	6	7	8	9
10	11	12	13	14	15	16
17	18	19	20	21	22	23
24	25	26	27	28	29	30

September

First Sunday

Life Changes

My son shared about two lives that define 2 Corinthians 5:17, "So if anyone is in Christ, there is a new creation: everything old has passed away; see everything has become new." He explained how this scripture truly came alive in teenage twin boys who had been expelled from their high school because of their troubled lives. Their problems included drug dealing, gang violence, jail time, lack of any work ethic or discipline, and a basic disrespect of others and themselves. There was no direction in their lives, and they were headed to prison, or worse. They were sent to an alternative school were my son worked. These twin brothers saw something different than their bad behavior in the life of my son. He also saw a potential in them; consequently, a life-changing relationship began. After spending considerable time together on Saturday mornings and before school, these boys began reading the Bible and asking questions. The words of Scripture seemed to bounce off the pages and into their hearts, and they wanted to learn more. What is this ancient book all about? Who is this man Jesus? What is God calling us to do with our lives? Can there be any real purpose for our life?

Eventually these boys came to know Christ and gave their lives in submission to their Lord and Savior. They both put their old ways of life behind them. After a great deal of mentoring, these boys applied for college, took the necessary exams, and both received full scholarships to a good university. These kinds of life changes were unheard of in their alternative school, as well as in the entire school district.

A news reporter could not understand what made the drastic change in the lives of these boys. What exactly happened? The reporter knew about the time spent in mentoring by the positive role model, but could not comprehend the behavioral changes in the twins. We know it was only Jesus Christ and the power of Divine love that changed the lives of these two young men.

The Apostle Paul wrote, "But God demonstrated His love toward us, in that, while we remained sinners, Christ died for us. Much more since, we are now justified by His blood; we shall be rescued from final punishment through Him. For if, when we were enemies, we were changed by the death of God's Son, much more, we are being changed by His life" (Romans 5:8-10). God loved us when we cared nothing about Him, and continually draws people to Himself, desiring a positive response toward Him. God can give us a new vision and hope for this life, and for the life to come.

When someone speaks about the time and commitment it takes to mentor troubled boys, my son humbly replies, "that is just what we are called to do: to invest in others and to point them to Jesus." This is true, but how often do we neglect to show others the love of Jesus with our time? The lives of many are going nowhere and are headed into trouble, and their lives are in need of great changes and direction. That is the objective of this Mission.

Let us not miss the opportunities to invest in the lives of those who desperately need Jesus, and simply do what we are called to do. It is good to work at this Mission where I am able to see my co-workers and volunteers invest in the lives of others on a daily basis, and see lives transformed through Jesus Christ.

NOTES AND REFLECTIONS

SEPTEMBER
SECOND SUNDAY

Since...

The Mission cook took her turn to reflect on Colossians 3:1-4 in recent staff devotions. Previously she asked a few people to write down their thoughts on this passage, so we could compare our thoughts on Paul's letter. Some did the "homework," and brought it to the meeting. Colossians 3:1 begins by saying, "Since..." The word "since" implies something preceded what the Apostle Paul was going to write, and indeed something did! "Since you are raised with Christ, keep on aspiring to heavenly things, where Christ is seated at the right hand of God." Christ seated at the right hand of God denotes authority and power, which Christ always had, but which He now had complete power even over death through His own resurrection.

Since we too are, "raised with Christ," He has given us all we need – we just need to use it! God has already done His work by giving us the Holy Spirit. We already have life in the Spirit, which enables us to live out the rest of this portion of Scripture: "Set your affections on heavenly things, not on earthly things. You have already undergone death and your new life is hid with Christ in God" (verses 2, 3). And what does "hid" in verse three mean? We are completely under the "wings" of protection of our Lord, where our lives are hid in His love and comfort. I think of the verse where Jesus said, "Jerusalem, Jerusalem, you who killed the prophets, and stone those who are sent to you, often would I have gathered your children together, as a hen gathers her chickens under her wings..." (Matthew 23:37; Luke 13:34).

The final verse of this section reads, "When Christ, our life returns, then shall you be illuminated with Him in triumph." What a wonderful promise! Christ truly is our life, and hidden under His wings, we have power from on high. Celebrate all Christ has made you to be!

When we begin our new life in Christ, we die to our old self as Paul wrote about in his letter, "Since you have stripped off the old nature and old practices, stop telling lies to one another; having put on the new nature, which is being freshly renewed in full knowledge in the likeness of the creator God." (Colossians 3:9)

Since God so generously gave us His Spirit, which provides the power to live sanctified lives, "Because the One who called you is holy, you must be holy in all manner of living; you must be holy because the scripture declares: God is holy!" (1 Peter 1:16).

NOTES AND REFLECTIONS

September

Third Sunday

New Lives for Old

When we become Christ followers, we are called to live holy, consecrated, sanctified lives, in other words, we are called to live new lives to replace our old ways of life. That does not mean that we need to get, "all cleaned up" and have our lives perfectly ordered before we acknowledge Christ and accept the life He has planned for us and the salvation He offers, but it does mean that in our faith walk, we need to rely on the Holy Spirit to begin the transforming work in our lives that only He can accomplish. As Christians, our lives do need to change, though not out of compulsion or rule-following, but out of love for our Savior and for others. We live better lives in response to the love and the far better lives God offers us.

1 Thessalonians 4:7-8 says, "For God did not call us on the basis of impurity but in the sphere of consecration. Therefore he who rejects this instruction does not reject man, but rejects the God, who gave us the Holy Spirit." What does it mean to live a holy or consecrated life? There are many places in the Bible that mention this idea, but I will focus on just a few familiar sections of scripture.

"Since you have stripped off the old nature and old practices, stop telling lies to one another; having put on the new nature, which is being freshly renewed in full knowledge in the likeness of the Creator God: as the consecrated, loved and select ones of God, clothe yourselves with a tender heart, kindness, humility, gentleness, and long-suffering; be generous with each other and overlook faults, forgiving all disagreements as Christ forgave you. In addition to all these put on compassionate love, which binds believers together in harmony." (Colossians 3:9-10,12-14).

The language of Colossians is similar to Galatians 5 which described the fruit of the Spirit, which reflect the life of a Christ-follower. Paul wrote to the Galatian church, "But the fruit of the Spirit is love, and love brings joy, peace, long-suffering, gentleness, goodness, faith, tolerance and self-control; and no law exists against any of these" (Galatians 5:22-23).

Paul wrote to the Christians in Ephesus, "I therefore, the prisoner in the Lord, implore you to behave worthy of the mission to which you are called, with humility and gentleness, patiently and lovingly bear with one another; giving diligence to maintain the unity of the Spirit in the alliance of peace" (Ephesians 4:1-3).

Some virtues of the sanctified, consecrated, or holy life overlap in Paul's letters to the Colossians, the Thessalonians, the Galatians and the Ephesians, so he must have thought them to be vital to the Christian life. He emphasized the importance of love, which binds them all together. In 1 Corinthians 13 Paul wrote that there are three important elements of the Christian life, faith, hope and love, "but the greatest of these is love" (1 Corinthians 13:13).

All of the virtues mentioned by Paul are also characteristics of Jesus, who reflects God the Father. As much as is humanly possible, we are to be imitators of Christ, asking the Holy Spirit to enable us to live out these virtues in love, and to live holy and sanctified lives, so that others may see the love of Jesus, and that His attributes are lived out in us. Paul wrote to Believers in Rome, "By His suffering we have exchanged our old life for new life at one with God." This week, as you read Scripture and reflect on the beautiful attributes of God, and the virtues He has called us to model, rejoice in your new life in Christ Jesus, the Redeemer.

NOTES AND REFLECTIONS

September

Fourth Sunday

What Really Counts

Danish philosopher and theologian Soren Kierkegaard (1813-1855), once wrote, "What really counts in life is that at some time you have seen something, felt something, which is so great, so matchless, that everything else is nothing by comparison, that even if you forgot everything, you would never forget this." In regards to this quote, some might think of a hauntingly beautiful piece of music, or an attractive piece of artwork. Some might think of something amazingly stunning in nature, such as the Grand Canyon or Victoria Falls, or an extremely colorful sunset. Others might think of a strong, close, loving relationship.

While art, music, nature, and relationships are indeed wonderful gifts God gives us for enjoyment, the Apostle Paul wrote similar in thought to Kierkegaard: "But what was once gain, I counted loss for Christ. Affirmative, I count all things but loss for the exceeding value of the knowledge of Christ Jesus my Lord: for Christ I suffered the loss of all things, and count them as manure, that I may win Christ" (Philippians 3:7-8).

As Christians, as Paul said, all else pales in this world compared to knowing, loving, and serving Christ Jesus; He is what really counts in life. Of course there are those who were not alive when Jesus walked this earth and have not seen Him, yet we have "seen" Him in His Word and in His Creation. "That which can be known of God lies plain before their minds. For the invisible qualities of God from the creation are clearly seen, being understood through the things God made, even his eternal power and Godhead." (Romans 1:19-20). We have felt God through the power of the Holy Spirit working through us, especially when in prayer, praise and worship. We have also felt God in the love received from Christian family and friends. Living in Christ is indeed "so great, so matchless," that like Kierkegaard echoed the words of Paul, "everything else is nothing," or is "manure" or "rubbish" in comparison.

Do you remember how you felt when you first acknowledged Jesus as your Lord and Savior? Do you remember the joy, the peace, the excitement of knowing that all of your past was wiped away, your sins were forgiven, and you were loved with a love that far exceeds any human love you may have experienced? Do you remember when you realized you would never really die, but that your eternity with Christ had already been initiated? Spiritual experience and faith in Christ is something we must never forget, because it is an ongoing component of our spiritual lives.

Even if we forget that wonderful musical score, or that beautiful piece of artwork, or that nature scene, or for some reason a once beautiful relationship ends, could we ever forget the wonderful experience of knowing the God of the universe, who created all of the beauty experienced in life? Yet, God became one of us, to bring us an abundant life, and an eternal life, free from sin and death.

Do we really consider, as Paul did, all else in life rubbish or manure? What about our house, our job, our education, our clothes, or our car? Does everything pale in comparison to our relationship with Jesus Christ? This week, as you listen to music, view a painting, study a sculpture, look at the beauty of Creation, or delight in a loving relationship, remember the God who gave all of these things. Reminisce about all the things that bring you joy and know that nothing you now experience will compare to God's love shed abroad in your heart by knowing Jesus Christ. And that nothing you experience will compare with the joy prepared for those who love God.

NOTES AND REFLECTIONS

October 2017

Sunday	Monday	Tuesday	Wednesday	Thursday	Friday	Saturday
1	2	3	4	5	6	7
8	9	10	11	12	13	14
15	16	17	18	19	20	21
22	23	24	25	26	27	28
29	30	31				

OCTOBER

FIRST SUNDAY

Two Wolves

There is an old Cherokee Indian Legend called the "Two Wolves," which focuses on the spiritual battles that take place inside all of us. One evening an old Cherokee told his grandson about this spiritual battle that goes on inside people during difficult times. He said, "My son, that battle is between two wolves inside of us all. One is Evil - it is anger, envy, jealousy, sorrow, regret, greed, arrogance, self-pity, resentment, inferiority, lies, pride, superiority and ego. The other is Good - it is joy, peace, love, hope, serenity, humility, kindness, benevolence, empathy, generosity, truth, compassion, trust and faith." The grandson thought about this for a moment, and then asked his grandfather, "Which wolf wins?" The old Cherokee simply replied, "The one you feed."

Solomon wrote in his old age, "For everything there is a season, and a time for every matter under heaven." (Ecclesiastes 3:1). We often hear this familiar chapter read at funerals, especially verse 4, "A time to weep and a time to laugh; a time to mourn and a time to dance." Would it not be nice if we just had times of laughter and dancing, and we could skip all the weeping and mourning parts? But life is filled with struggles, challenges and sadness at various times, which can negatively affect our spiritual walk with

Christ. How do difficult times affect spiritual matters of the soul and the strength of our faith? What becomes our focus when we are hit with bad news such as illness, financial difficulties, betrayal, injustice, or the death of a loved one? In times like these, were do our thoughts go?

Paul beautifully told us where to keep our thoughts when he wrote, "Whatever is true, whatever is honorable, whatever is just, whatever is pure, whatever is pleasing, whatever is commendable, if there is any excellence and if there is anything worthy of praise, think about these things" (Philippians 4:8-9 NRSV). The question is, can we think about "these things" in the midst of pain and difficulty? How do we deal with the spiritual battles that we face when life hurts, when Satan is trying to rob us of spiritual joy and shake the foundations of our faith?

The fruit of the Spirit as found in Galatians 5:22-26 is love, and the others: joy, peace, patience, kindness, meekness and self-control come from love. This week, meditate on Philippians 4:8-9 and see where your thoughts and focus lie, thinking about which wolf you feed, and see which wolf inside of YOU is winning.

NOTES AND REFLECTIONS

OCTOBER

SECOND SUNDAY

The Harvest

A saying attributed to Saint Francis said, "Preach the Gospel always, and if necessary, use words." Since this saying did not emerge until two centuries after Saint Francis lived, there is a good chance he never actually said it; but is this quote really how we should live our lives?

It is necessary that as Christ-followers we reflect the life and teachings of Jesus, and out of love we should bear good fruit and "preach" the gospel with our lives. Words however, are also extremely important. The last words Jesus spoke on earth were, "All authority has been committed to Me in heaven and in earth. As you personally go, therefore, and make disciples of all nations, baptizing them in the name of the Father, and of the Son, and of the Holy Spirit: teaching them to observe all things whatever I have commanded you..." (Matthew 28:18-20). Jesus said to "make disciples and teach," which does require both lifestyle and words of witness.

What happens when we simply think our lifestyle, good deeds, and kindness alone will "preach the gospel" and we say nothing? People who do not know Jesus will remain ignorant of God's plan of salvation unless we "teach" them the plan. There are many kind people who do good deeds, who do not even believe in God, and have no knowledge of Jesus' saving Atonement. We need both lifestyle and "words."

A volunteer at the Mission was recently killed. He was a likeable young man, who did community service hours at the Mission, mandated by the court. I was personally kind, but never shared the Gospel with him. Did he know Jesus? Not knowing haunts me.

Several years ago, a wonderful and kind elderly neighbor's wife died, and after 60 years of marriage, he was lost without her. We shared dinner once a week, and took in church dinners and concerts, and although he was invited he declined Sunday services. I never preached the Gospel using words, mistakenly thinking my being a good neighbor was enough. I thought I was "preaching" the gospel to my neighbor by my actions, without specific words, but one day, he killed himself. Did he know Jesus? Again, the uncertainty troubles me.

"For everyone who calls upon the name of the Lord shall be saved. How shall they call on Him in whom they have not learned to believe? And how shall they believe in Him of whom they have never heard? And how shall they hear without a messenger?" (Romans 10:13-14). We must also preach the gospel with words so others will understand how to know Jesus, the forgiveness He offers, and life He wants Believers to live.

Jesus told His disciples, "The harvest is truly abundant, but the workers are few" (Matthew 9:37; Luke 10:2). We need to be workers. Is it enough to just live the gospel without words and never "preach the gospel" with words? A Muslim once asked a missionary, "Since Christians truly believe Jesus is the only way to Heaven, why aren't they out telling everyone?" Good question...

NOTES AND REFLECTIONS

OCTOBER

THIRD SUNDAY

Sheep to the Slaughter

A recent fire drill during staff meeting at the Mission taught us that we were not adequately informed. All but four people walked out the wrong door, and walked past two doors of the room that was "burning" during the drill. We even opened two fire doors that would have contained a real fire, keeping people on the other side of the building safe. Not only would we have jeopardized our own safety, but also the safety of others, had there been an actual fire. Thankfully, this was a "safety drill" only and not a fire!

We were briefed on why the chosen exit was wrong and risky, as we had just followed the person in front of us. Philosopher Eric Hoffer wrote "When people are free to do as they please, they usually imitate each other." We need to ensure when others imitate us, we are acting Christ-like and that we are not simply following the crowd, moving in the wrong direction.

The comment was made about "herd mentality," which brought to mind Isaiah 53:6: "All we like sheep have gone astray; we have all turned to our own way, and the Lord has laid on him the iniquity of us all." It is sad to admit how easy it was to follow co-workers, without thinking, perhaps because there was no real danger since it was just a drill. Most turned to their way, not taking the correct path that would have led out of the building, away from the "fire," and any danger. Many live their lives in such a manner: following others, not really thinking, or realizing that the path they are traveling does not lead to Jesus, and their path will eventually lead them to real danger.

"Death comes from being carnally minded; but to be spiritually minded is life and peace."(Romans 8:6). Are we controlled by our own desires and carnal thoughts, or rather controlled by God's Holy Spirit? Do we ever get caught up in the world and the things around us, following the crowd, rather than the words of Scripture? Do we know the Bible well enough to realize whether we are walking on the right path, following Scripture, and heading in the right direction? "They have all turned aside from the right path" (Romans 3:11-12).

During the fire drill, most did indeed turn aside from the right path and followed a path that could have led to destruction, had there been a real fire. "There is a way that seems right to a person, but its end is the way to death." (Proverbs 14:12). If we are walking down a path that is not in line with Scripture, then we are not on the right path. Whatever we do, whatever decisions we make, and wherever we go in this life, we must always follow the path of righteousness, taught in the Bible; any other path will lead us into danger and eventually death.

If the "herd mentality" is followed, we must make sure the Shepherd is Jesus. Most of us know Psalm 23, "The Lord is my shepherd, I shall not want. He makes me lie down in green pastures; he leads me beside still waters; he restores my soul. He leads me in right paths for his name's sake." Isaiah wrote that we are indeed as sheep that have all gone astray, but our Lord desires to be the True Shepherd, and lead us in the right path.

NOTES AND REFLECTIONS

October

Fourth Sunday

Loss with Hope

As a former hospice chaplain and bereavement counselor, I dealt with many deaths, including, the loss when a loved one dies. Probably the most painful loss is the death of loved ones, but throughout life we deal with the loss of jobs, homes, health, status, finances, relationships, and even roles such as provider, business owner, or spouse. Clients at the Mission experience many hurts and sorrows, including many of those listed above. Some have lost respect of their families, and even self-respect, due to addictions and multiple poor choices. One of the saddest wounds to see is the loss of hope.

Any loss listed is indeed legitimate and causes grief. We should empathize with those who experience loss, but what does the Bible have to say concerning loss? St. Paul wrote in his letter to the Philippians, "But what was once gain I counted loss for Christ. Affirmative, I count all things but loss for the exceeding value of the knowledge of Christ Jesus my Lord: for Christ I suffered the loss of all things..." (Philippians 3:7-8 a). In comparison to knowing Christ, nothing else even comes close to such a precious gift. Are we willing to forsake all, if necessary, to embrace Christ and Him crucified? Paul wrote in his letter to the Galatian church, "I have been crucified with Christ: nevertheless I live, yet not I, but Christ lives in me: and the life I now live in the flesh I live by the faith of the Son of God, who loved me, and gave Himself for me" (Galatians 2:20). Jesus willingly gave up everything because of His love for us. Jesus gave up the glory of Heaven to come down to earth, become man, while remaining fully God, and then gave His life so that we can have eternal life, beginning today. Jesus is calling us to give up everything for the sake of knowing Him, which is the greatest joy and fulfillment we can experience in this life.

In John 3:30, John the Baptist said, "Jesus must grow greater, but I must decrease." In other words, we are to decrease ourselves in order for Christ to increase and work through us. According to the Bible, when we experience loss, we never need to lose hope, but we can actually find hope when we turn towards Jesus. Paul wrote in his letter to the Thessalonian church, "I do not want you to remain in the dark about the believers who are asleep, (dead) that you sorrow not as others who have no hope" (I Thessalonians 4:13). As believers in Jesus Christ, when we lose everything, even the lives of loved ones, we still live with hope.

There is a story in the Old Testament about Job, who lost everything: his children, his health, his livestock, his servants, his wealth, literally everything except his life. How did Job respond? He said, "Naked I came from my mother's womb, and naked shall I return. The Lord gave, and the Lord has taken away; blessed be the name of the Lord" (Job 1:21). I cannot imagine anyone, including myself, saying those words of Job in the midst of such great loss, yet by the grace of God, Job did.

If you are in the midst of pain due to loss in your life, take hope in Christ, who walks with you through your sufferings. He can fully empathize with you in time of need, and He will restore your joy and hope, just as he replaced Job's loss.

NOTES AND REFLECTIONS

OCTOBER

FIFTH SUNDAY

Sainthood

All Saints Day is celebrated by Catholics and some Protestants on November 1, but the vigil of the celebration is on October 31, commonly known as All Hallows Eve or Halloween. Hallow is an Old English word when used as a noun, means saint, but when used as a verb, means to honor something as holy. All Saints Day arose from the tradition that celebrated the martyrdom of saints which increased during the late Roman Empire. Local dioceses instituted a common Feast Day to ensure that all martyrs, known and unknown were honored. November 1, was instituted by Pope Gregory III (731-741), when he consecrated a chapel to all the martyrs in St. Peter's Basilica and ordered an annual celebration. Some Protestant traditions do not celebrate All Saints Day, but we should remember the Heroes of Faith who went before to prepare the way for us.

What does the Bible teach about sainthood? The Bible does acknowledge "saints" as those who believe and love the Lord. Psalm 34:9 recorded, "Fear the Lord, you his saints..." and Psalm 30:4: "Sing to the Lord, you saints of his; praise his holy name." Also, Psalm 149:1, "Praise the Lord. Sing to the Lord a new song, his praise in the assembly of the saints." God's people, gathered together in praise and worship are His saints. In the letter to the

Ephesian Church, Paul acknowledged the congregations'
love for the Lord and also for the saints in chapter 1 verse
15, and told them to pray for the saints in Ephesians 6:18. In
Paul's letter to Philemon he also wrote, "It has been a joyful
comfort to me, brother, to hear of the refreshment you have
brought to the hearts of the saints" (verse 7). Revelation
speaks of the prayers of the saints in chapter 5 verse 8 and
of the righteousness of the saints in 19:8.

Protestants and Catholics may define sainthood
differently, but the Bible does indeed talk about saints.
The tradition of honoring the "saints" who have been
martyred years ago during the Roman Empire, as well as
those Christians who have been martyred in recent days,
can be a meaningful practice; so can honoring the "saints"
in your own church who have gone on to be with Jesus
be meaningful as well. If you are in a church who already
carries on this tradition, or in a church who has never
practiced this tradition, we can still set aside a time this
week to remember and honor our brothers and sisters in the
Lord who have been martyred for the Faith, as well as for
those who have died in other ways, who have walked this
earth in service to our Lord.

NOTES AND REFLECTIONS

November 2017

Sunday	Monday	Tuesday	Wednesday	Thursday	Friday	Saturday
			1	2	3	4
5	6	7	8	9	10	11
12	13	14	15	16	17	18
19	20	21	22	23	24	25
26	27	28	29	30		

November
First Sunday

The Bible

What is so special about the Bible that we need to read it each day? What separates the Bible from any other book? The Bible is the place where God chooses to reveal Himself, and the primary place where He speaks to us. Apart from the Bible, a person cannot really know God or have any understanding of the Christian faith. The Bible is the only reliable account that we have of the life of Jesus written by eye witnesses such as His disciples.

The Old Testament reveals the Holy and Perfect nature of God, and teaches about Creation, human nature, sin, forgiveness, and points the way to Jesus, the long-awaited Messiah. This allows us to recognize Him as Savior when we reach the New Testament. "All sacred writings are God-breathed, and serviceable for teaching, for warning, for correction, for instruction in righteousness, in order that the man of God may be adequately equipped for every good work." (II Timothy 3:16-17). In other words, Paul is telling us that the Bible is the only place to go for understanding of the correct way to live, and the words are breathed out by God Himself. Some may have heard the story of a small boy being asked the meaning of the B.I.B.L.E. His answer was short and snappy: the Bible means, "Basic Instructions Before Leaving Earth."

In the letter to the Ephesians, Paul wrote about spiritual warfare, and that we must be ready to fight by putting on the whole armor of God which is essential in the battle against Satan and evil. Paul wrote, "Finally, my brothers, be strengthened in the Lord, and in the power of His unlimited resource. Wear the complete armor of God, so you can stand against the strategy and assault of the adversary. For our wrestling is not against a physical enemy, but against evil princes of darkness, who rule this world, and against hosts of spiritual wickedness in heavenly warfare. Wherefore wear the complete armor of God that you may be able to withstand evil attacks when they come, and be found still standing. Stand your ground, being protected by Truth, and having integrity for a breastplate; and the gospel of peace preparing your feet for battle, above all, take the shield of faith to extinguish all the fiery darts of the wicked. And take the helmet of salvation, and the sword of the Spirit, which is the word of God" (Ephesians 6:10-17).

Even Jesus used the Word of God when He was battling Satan in the wilderness. In Matthew 4:1-11 and again in Luke 4:1-13, Satan tempted Jesus three times, and the only weapon Jesus fought back with was the Holy Scripture. With each temptation that Satan used, Jesus quoted the words of the Old Testament book of Deuteronomy saying, "The Scripture says..." (Luke 4:4), and "It is written... (Luke 4:7) and finally, "For it is written..." (Luke 4:10). Jesus knew the power of God's Word. Satan also used Scripture against Jesus, quoting from Psalm 91, but blatantly misused it in an effort to try and manipulate Jesus; of course Jesus knew the Scriptures too well to fall into Satan's trap. When we do not know the Scripture it is easy for Satan and/or non-believers to manipulate us.

If we claim to be Christ-followers, to know and love God as our Lord and Savior, but do not take the time each day to hear from Him, get to know Him more, and learn from Him, we have no chance in our fight against the "prince of this world" who will trick us, manipulate us, and eventually defeat us. If Jesus Himself needed Scripture in His battle, how much more do we? This week, take some time each day, and develop a daily reading schedule, asking the Holy Spirit to reveal God to you on a deeper level, and He will.

NOTES AND REFLECTIONS

November

Second Sunday

Heaven and Hell

Most of us know Matthew 25, where Jesus said that when we feed others, give a drink to others, welcome strangers, clothe those in need, care for the sick, visit people in prison, that we are doing these things as unto Him. This passage also says that if we fail to do these things for others, we fail to do these things for Christ. The Christian faith is a faith built in community, and when we worship and live in community, we are truly functioning as the Body of Christ that Scripture mandates. In 1 Corinthians 12, Paul wrote of the various gifts given to us in order to work together as a functioning Body that serves Christ and also enables us to serve one another as Christ intended.   The focus of life should never be on self or to serve personal needs, but rather in focusing on the needs of others.

There is an old short story called the "Allegory of Long Spoons," which is attributed to Rabbi Haim of Romshishok, but is folklore in many cultures, including Jewish, Hindu, Buddhist and Christian. This allegory is not found in the Bible, but it certainly has biblical principles about caring for other people as Matthew 25 commands.

Upon his death, a man was given a tour of both Heaven and Hell, so he could see what his final destination might be like. First he was taken to Hell. He saw a lot of people sitting at a long banquet table loaded with all kinds of delicious foods. However, he noticed that all of the people seated were unhappy and looked frustrated. They each had a spoon strapped to their left arms and a knife strapped to their right arms. Each had a four foot handle which made it impossible for them to eat.

With all kinds of delicious foods in front on the table, the starving guests were unable to taste any of it. After this scene in Hell, he was taken on a tour of Heaven and noticed that the people in Heaven were also seated at a long banquet table with all kinds of delicious foods. However, there was a difference here in Heaven because he noticed that the people were cheerful and enjoying themselves. They also had spoons and knives strapped to their arms with four foot handles, but they were busy eating and enjoying their food because they were feeding each other. Each person in Heaven was feeding the person across the table, and in turn was being fed by the person across the table. The people in Hell on the other hand, were unable to eat and went hungry because they were only trying to feed themselves.

This week may God give you opportunities to live out Matthew 25, and may we as Christians grow in the Body of Christ, without dissension, as we reach across the banquet table of life and feed one another.

NOTES AND REFLECTIONS

NOVEMBER

THIRD SUNDAY

Thankfulness

This week most of us will celebrate Thanksgiving, probably my favorite holiday. What a wonderful privilege we have to set a full day aside to be with family and/or friends, or to serve a dinner somewhere, simply to think about how blessed we are and what we have to be thankful for. The Apostle Paul wrote, "Always rejoice in the Lord: and again I will say, rejoice. Let your gentleness be known to everyone. The Lord is at hand. Be anxious for nothing; but under all circumstances by general prayer and specific petition joined with thanksgiving let your personal needs be known to God. And the authentic peace of God, which surpasses all comprehension, will guard your hearts and minds in Christ Jesus." (Philippians 4:4-7).

It is difficult to rejoice and give thanks always. As we pray and make petitions known to God, we must do so with thanksgiving and faith, even before we know the outcome. It is easy to rejoice and give thanks when life is good and we are satisfied, but it is not easy to be thankful when things do not go our way. "In everything give thanks; for this is the desire of God in Christ Jesus concerning you." (I Thessalonians 5:18). How often have you prayed for something and not received, only to find out later that God had something much better for you? It is easy to give thanks in those situations, in retrospect, but how often do we give thanks during those difficult times?

Many Christian friends in Kenya say they possess very little, that their lives are difficult, but that they are thankful to have such a loving God who loves and cares for them, and has granted them salvation. Have you noticed that the less people have materially and financially, the more grateful and generous they are? Thankfulness is truly an act of the will, and is not dependent on circumstances.

Most in America will share a Thanksgiving dinner with family and friends. Others will spend Thanksgiving serving at a Mission and providing a dinner for those who are less fortunate and who may not have anywhere to go for the holiday. Some may be those who have nowhere to go, but are thankful to be served. How truly blessed we are, in whatever position we find ourselves, to set aside a day to share a meal and give thanks with family and friends. We all must be thankful, not so much for what we have, but for a loving God who is merciful beyond measure. He loved us and sent His Son to die for us and provide eternal life for those who believe.

This week, as you may take some time to celebrate Thanksgiving, remember to give thanks in all things, for this is the will of Christ Jesus. And most of all, give thanks that we have a God who so wondrously loves us and has promised to always be with us.

NOTES AND REFLECTIONS

November

Fourth Sunday

Advent

This week begins the four weeks leading up to Christmas, which in the liturgical calendar year is called Advent. The word "Advent" comes from the Latin, "adventus," which means "coming," and extrapolates from the Greek word "parousia." Advent is a time of preparation and anticipation for the coming, or birth of Jesus Christ. Not all Christians follow the liturgical calendar, but as a Believer I celebrate Advent because of the beauty of living life in the rhythm and cycle of the Christian faith. I celebrate the life, death, and resurrection of Jesus together with other Christians.

The Gospels described how Mary, the Mother of Jesus, was told by the Angel Gabriel that she would conceive the Savoir of the world through the Holy Spirit and bear a Son who, "shall be well-known, and be called the Son of the Highest: and the Lord God shall give him the throne of his forefather David: and he will reign over the house of Jacob forever, and his reign shall have no end" (Luke 1:32-33).

Luke 1:46-55 shared Mary's song of praise, or what is known as "The Magnificat" when she pondered the upcoming birth of the Christ Child. When the holiday season gets hectic, do we complain about all that needs to be done during this busy time or as Mary, do we sing a song of praise and prepare with anticipation the birth of the Savior, God Incarnate, and Emmanuel: God with us?

While we busily prepare for Christmas, do we grasp "Who" it was that came into the world to save sinners? What exactly are we celebrating? Are we caught up in the secularization of this most holy time of the year? How often have you heard someone say, "I can't wait for Christmas to be over!" Why not say "I can't wait until the blessed event that celebrates the birth of Christ." We must minimize the stress that logically comes with this most wonderful time of year.

Perhaps this year we could concentrate more on the Christ Child who came into the world for the redemption and salvation of those who accept His love. This would enable parents and/or grandparents to make a "perfect Christmas." When large families have so many gifts to buy, parties to host and/or attend, cards to mail, homes to decorate, and sugar cookies to bake, it becomes easy to permit the stress to rob them of the joy of Christmas.

I am also reminded of the story in Luke about Martha and her sister Mary (not Jesus' mother), who welcomed Jesus into their home. While Mary was sitting at the Lord's feet listening to His teachings, Martha complained that she was busy running around serving and her sister was not helping. "Jesus answered, 'Martha, Martha, you are anxious and burdened about many things: but one thing is needful: and Mary has chosen the good part, and it will not be taken from her'" (Luke 10:41). Let us choose the "good part" of Christmas. We could sing a song of praise as Mary did or choose the "good part" and listen at the feet of Jesus the true story of Christmas. Then the most important part of the Holiday Season, the Celebration of the Birth of the Messiah would be the blessed event in each heart and home.

NOTES AND REFLECTIONS

December 2017

Sunday	Monday	Tuesday	Wednesday	Thursday	Friday	Saturday
					1	2
3	4	5	6	7	8	9
10	11	12	13	14	15	16
17	18	19	20	21	22	23
24 31	25	26	27	28	29	30

December

First Sunday

Always Enough Time to Pray

Prayer is important; yet many neglect this vital part of the Christian life and succumb to a busy festive season rather than making Christmas a Festival of Faith.   Faith and the biblical story must be a central part of the Holiday Season. Artificial festivities and a party spirit must never replace the true reason for the season. Business is an excuse; not an explanation or justification for the neglect of spiritual matters.

Even Jesus, God's Perfect Man, knew the value of prayer and took time to pray, "And Jesus arose while it was still dark and departed into a private place to pray." (Mark 1:35). When Jesus knew He was about to suffer betrayal, and death, He knew the critical value of prayer, "And they" (the disciples) "came to a place called Gethsemane: and Jesus said to His disciples, Sit here while I pray" (Mark 14:32). These demonstrate the importance Jesus placed on prayer - on His communing with the Father!

As a leader, Samuel said to his people, "Far be it from me that I should sin against the Lord by ceasing to pray for you" (1 Samuel 12:23). He actually called neglected prayer a sin! Do we pray daily for those we serve, those where we work, those with whom we worship and fellowship, and perhaps most importantly, those with whom we live? "Acknowledge your failures and side steps to one another, and pray for yourselves and for one another, that you may be made spiritually whole again." (James 5:16). Many know the verse II Chronicles 7:14 "If my people, who are called by my name humble themselves, pray, seek my face, and turn from their wicked ways, then I will hear from Heaven, and will forgive their sin and heal their land." God said and Jesus modeled prayer as a crucial part of life. Paul wrote "pray without ceasing" (1 Thessalonians 5:17).

Some talk about going into their "prayer closets" to pray, meaning make the space and time to pray. The chorus of an old hymn speaks volumes about prayer:

> *"Shut in with God in a secret place*
> *There in the spirit, beholding His face*
> *Gaining new power to run in this race*
> *Oh, I love to be shut in with God."*

If Jesus felt the need to pray, how can we neglect the ministry of prayer? Seminary students in Kenya where I served would rise early and pray for hours before starting the day. One Kenyan friend made a "prayer room" in his home to pray each morning. Would we consider getting up at 4:00 a.m. just to pray before we began a long day? Do we really understand the value of prayer?

This is not a suggestion that we get up at 4:00 each morning to pray, but perhaps this week we can make a more concerted effort to take time to pray daily. May God bless you in the spiritual discipline of prayer, no matter how busy life becomes this week. Beware the bareness of a busy life. The emptiness of life demands prayer. The busier you are, the more necessary prayer becomes.

NOTES AND REFLECTIONS

DECEMBER

SECOND SUNDAY

Prince of Peace

"For a child has been born for us, a son given to us; authority rests upon his shoulders; and he is named Wonderful Counselor, Mighty God, Everlasting Father, Prince of Peace" (Isaiah 9:6). We read this verse around the Christmas season, and most scholars believe Isaiah was describing the coming Messiah - Jesus, as the Messianic King. The authority of the Messiah is His symbol of power. The Wonderful Counselor is the wisdom and perfect teachings of Jesus. The Mighty God is Jesus as both fully divine and at the same time fully human - God Incarnate. The Everlasting Father is the loving care of our Heavenly Father, and the Prince of Peace is the King who will ultimately bring peace to the world.

Unfortunately, we do not see the world peace that this King will bring, but we know that Jesus, the Messianic King "shall be the one of peace" (Micah 5:5 b) as the Old Testament prophets foretold. When we read the Christmas story about the birth of baby Jesus, the Angel and the Heavenly Host were praising God, "Glory to God on high and peace on earth to men of good will" (Luke 2:14). How we long for peace on earth; yet from the Garden Fall, until the present, the world has not experienced this peace. So, to what does this peace refer? Perhaps as we approach

Christmas, we can think of the Christ-Child, Baby Jesus, as the Prince of Peace who came to make peace between God and mankind. We, as believers, know that through the coming of Jesus, we now have personal peace with God, even though we often stray as sheep far from Him. Because of His great love for us, we can be at peace with God. In Jesus "All the fullness of God was pleased to dwell, and through him God was pleased to reconcile to himself all things, whether on earth or in Heaven, by making peace through the blood of his cross" (Colossians 1:19-20, NRSV).

While we may not experience world peace as we see wars, terrorism, violence, etc. each day, we can know that our great King, the Messiah, Jesus, is the True Prince of Peace and has come as a small baby to bring ultimate peace and reconciliation between man and God, despite our sins, if only we believe and accept His most precious gift. We can find rest and peace for our souls, despite the unrest and violence of the world. Ultimately when King Jesus returns in His glory, He will indeed usher in a world of everlasting and eternal peace. Until then, Jesus said, "Peace I leave with you, My peace I give to you: but not as the world gives. Let not your heart be troubled, neither fearful" (John 14:27).

With the multiplication of gifts we give and receive this Christmas season, let us remember the greatest gift of all - peace with God and salvation through Christ. This week, embrace the gift of Jesus, and while earthly peace may be lacking, we can experience the peace that Jesus, the Prince of Peace brings to believers. Remember, that the "authentic peace of God which transcends all comprehension shall guard your hearts and minds through Christ Jesus" (Philippians 4:7).

NOTES AND REFLECTIONS

DECEMBER

THIRD SUNDAY

In the Image of God

We hear more about Mary, the mother of Jesus, during the Christmas season, than at any other time. The Council of Ephesus decreed in 431 that Mary was the "Theotokos" because her son Jesus was God in the flesh; one Divine Person with two natures (Divine and human) intimately, hypostatically united. In the Greek, "Theo" means God, and "tokos" means to bring forth or to bear. Mary was consequently called the "God-bearer," because she literally bore the Son of God in the flesh!

Mary had a humble attitude, a loving heart, and an amazing faith. In Luke 1 the Angel Gabriel visited Mary to tell her that she had, "Found favor with God" and that she would bear His Son through the power of the Holy Spirit. Mary was young, a virgin, and not yet married, yet she still responded to Gabriel by saying, "Here am I, the servant of the Lord; let it be according to your word" (Luke 1:38 NRSV). Mary was given confusing, even frightening words by the Angel, yet she responded with such amazing faith. Since she was not yet married to Joseph, Mary could have been stoned by Jewish Law when her pregnancy was discovered and Joseph had not believed her explanation. Was he not ready to call off the wedding? "But Joseph, her promised husband, being honorable and unwilling to expose her publically, considered how to handle the matter secretly" (Matthew 1:19). Fortunately, "a messenger of the Lord appeared to him in a dream, saying, Joseph, child of David, do not fear to take Mary as your wife, for the child within her was conceived by the Holy Spirit" (Matthew 1:20). That angelic announcement to Joseph must have stretched his faith.

When Mary, a young pregnant girl visited her older cousin, Elizabeth, soon to be the mother of John the Baptist, Mary shared what is now called "The Magnificat." Mary said, "My soul over-flows with praise to the Lord, and my spirit delights in God my Savior. For He has graciously regarded his humble servant: just watch, henceforth all generations shall call me blessed" (Luke 1:46-48). How many young girls in the same situation today would respond as Mary did understanding the possible consequences? Yet, we are all called to live our lives in faith, regardless of circumstances, and to be obedient to God's Will.

We are all made in the image of God and are to display that image daily. Mary was the actual God-bearer, the "Theotokos," but we too are called to bear the image of God in all aspects of our lives. Believers should ask the Holy Spirit daily to live through us in such a way that others can see Jesus in us.

During this Christmas season, we should all seek to manifest the faith of Mary and Joseph. They both responded to trials, difficulties and the unknown and declared: "let it be according to Your Word."

NOTES AND REFLECTIONS

DECEMBER

FOURTH SUNDAY

The Banquet

Most of the staff and many volunteers will be at our annual Lexington Rescue Mission banquet. In regards to some of our guests, our Mission clients, I thought of Jesus' teaching in Luke 14, where Scripture says, "When you give a banquet, invite the poor, the crippled, the lame, the blind, and you will be blessed. Although they cannot repay you, you will be repaid at the resurrection of the righteous" (Luke 14:13-14). What a joy it is to have some of our clients briefly tell their stories of how their lives were transformed through the Rescue Mission. However, we need to keep in mind that their lives were not changed through the Mission itself, or even through any of us, but their lives were changed by the power of the Gospel of Jesus Christ; we are merely the vessels God uses to draw people to Him. Seeing lives transformed is indeed such a joy, and what an honor to have a night where we can share that joy with others.

We will get all dressed up and ready to go after much preparation has been done and the night is finally here. But what if no preparations had been made or no planning had gone into this event? What if no one showed up? Jesus is preparing a banquet for us, that we need to prepare and dress for when the time comes. Will we be ready? Are we preparing for His banquet? Jesus told a parable of the banquet He has planned for us that is recorded in Matthew 22:1-14: A king prepared a banquet for his son and invited many people. The food was all prepared and the invitations sent out, but people paid no attention, ignored the king, and did not attend, so the king told his servants to go out to the street corners and invite whoever they could find, "both good and bad" and the banquet hall was then filled. However, one guest came without the proper clothing (which we assume would have been supplied by the king's servants), ignoring the order of the king, and this ill-prepared person was thrown out of the banquet hall. What does this parable teach? God has been preparing the Wedding Supper of the Lamb for us to share in from the beginning of time. He is inviting us all, and we need to accept His invitation. We also need to clothe ourselves with the clothing God provides for us through Jesus Christ. We will be given robes of righteousness that Revelation 19:7-8 speaks of: "Let us be glad and rejoice, and give honor to Him: for the marriage day of the Lamb has come, and His bride has made herself ready. And to her was granted that she should be arrayed in fine linen, clean and white: for the fine linen is the righteousness of saints."

As we prepare for our Mission banquet, let us be grateful that there is indeed wonderful food to eat, we have proper clothing to wear, a beautiful banquet hall has been made ready, and we can bring praise and honor to our Lord and Savior who changes lives. He is preparing us for His banquet, the Wedding Supper of the Lamb, and during our lifetime, let us make the necessary preparations and invite all those of whom we meet.

NOTES AND REFLECTIONS

December

Fifth Sunday

Resolutions

It is time to close out one year and begin another. Some make New Year's resolutions and a few actually follow through with their pledges, while most do not. Go to any gym to work out in January, and it will be crowded. As the months go by, that resolution of daily exercise begins to wain and the gyms become empty. People say they are going to eat healthier, lose weight, get in shape, etc., but never stick to the new diet and exercise plan. While those are all great health related resolutions, we need more promises about spiritual health. Occasionally, some say they are going to read the Bible daily, or read spiritual books or attend church regularly; these are good resolutions, but the resolutions are only "good" if they are kept.

The Apostle Paul wrote to Timothy, "Train yourself in godliness, for, while physical training is of some value, godliness is valuable in every way, holding promise for both the present life and for the life to come" (1 Timothy 4:7-8 NRSV). This sounds like a great New Year's resolution! Simon Peter said that we can indeed train in godliness; he wrote, "His divine power has given us everything needed for life and godliness, through the knowledge of him who called us by his own glory and godliness." (2 Peter 1:3 NRSV). Peter continued that we can even "share the divine nature" (2 Peter 1:4 b), but only through the grace of God and the working of the Holy Spirit can we live godly lives and participate in the divine nature. We cannot become godly people through our own efforts, no matter how hard we try, but we must depend on the Holy Spirit to empower us to reach these levels of spiritual maturity. Trying to be godly will not last, just as so many of New Year's resolutions which soon fall by the way side.

Peter continued his thought by writing, "You must make every effort to support your faith with goodness, and goodness with knowledge, and knowledge with self-control, and self-control with endurance, and endurance with godliness, and godliness with mutual affection, and mutual affection with love" (2 Peter 1:5-7 NRSV). Personal faith comes first, it is a gift from God, and then we must live in faith by these "efforts" that only God can equip us to maintain faith, as we grow in the grace and knowledge of God.

Since the Bible is the place where God reveals Himself, it is crucial that we are in the Word each day, learning to walk and trust God. It is vital that we pray each day and open our hearts and minds to listen to our Heavenly Father. Paul wrote to the Corinthian Church, "Therefore if any man be in Christ, he is a new creation: observe, the old things have passed away; all things have become new. All thing are from God, who has brought us together in Himself by Christ Jesus, and has given to us the ministry of bringing people together, how that God was in Christ bringing together the world to Himself" (2 Corinthians 5:17-19 a). In Christ, we "put on the new nature, which is being freshly renewed in full knowledge in the likeness of the Creator God" (Colossians 3:10).

This week think about New Year's resolutions, pray for God's loving grace to shower you with His Spirit and enable you to grow in the knowledge of Christ and live a godly life. I trust your New Year's resolutions are those you can keep. Then, you will grow in grace and knowledge of God and live a godly life in Christ Jesus.

NOTES AND REFLECTIONS

ABOUT THE AUTHOR

Donna (Kasik) Junker is a native of the Chicago suburbs. While attending college (where she received an under graduate degree in Philosophy) and seminary at night for many years, she owned her own business in the

construction trades. After receiving the Master of Divinity, she moved to Kentucky, then several different states to complete her Clinical Pastoral Education.

Donna worked as a hospice Chaplain for a decade. Her current position is Chaplain/Pastoral Care Coordinator with the Lexington Rescue Mission in Lexington, Kentucky. She is ordained through the World Council of Independent Christian Churches (WCICC). Her passion is cultural studies and mission work. She taught short-term intensives at a seminary in Kenya, East Africa, for 6 years, ministered at Mother Teresa's home for the dying in Calcutta, India, and worked at an AIDS hospice in Zambia, Southern Africa.

Donna is married to Dr. Paul Junker. She loves to travel, read, write, cook, run, the Arts, and all outdoor activities. She is active in her community and local church, and served in the Ministerial Association. Donna has one son, of whom she is very proud, and a wonderful daughter-in-law. She has become a doting grandmother to a delightful little girl and a great step-grandson. Her greatest joy in life is being a follower of Jesus Christ, who brings peace that passes understanding, along with joy and contentment that the world could never give.

"The Lexington Rescue Mission in Lexington, Kentucky is a wonderful place that provides spiritual care and serves hot and nutritious meals to the poor and homeless in the community. Also, the Mission provides clothing, blankets, sleeping bags, toiletries, emergency utility, rent assistance, bus passes, transitional housing for those released from prison and/or recovering from addictions, job training, life skills, and re-entry programs for those coming out of prison. Those interested in the Lexington Rescue Mission, may go to *www. LexingtonRescue.org* and learn about the Mission, their history, financials, staff, Statement of Faith, social services, volunteer opportunities, special events, how to contact or donate to the Mission, or to follow their Blog."

BOOKS BY THE AUTHOR

The first four books listed were published under the author's Maiden name: Donna Kasik.

Three Weeks in Africa
ISBN: 978-1-935434-13-9

"We as the American hospices are not sent to help the poor African hospices, but to deepen relationships with them, to assess needs and to discover how they function. We can share our knowledge with them, and they in turn can share their knowledge and insight with us." Hospice and Palliative Care is a new concept in Africa, and is established, funded and carried out in different ways than American hospices. The author's 3-pronged purpose in writing this book is to: 1) Approach hospice care from a missional point of view, 2) Share the importance of compassionate, faith-based end-of-life care, and 3) Understand and appreciate Zambia's challenges of hospice and palliative care.

Kenya: A Priority on My Bucket List
ISBN: 978-1-935434-63-4

A list of things to do or accomplish before exiting this life is called a bucket list. One of the items on the author's bucket list was to go somewhere in Africa to see the wild animals in their natural habitat. Little did she know that Kenya, East Africa would become like a second home and would offer far more than a safari ride. Traveling to Kenya seven times, the author gives a detailed account of her experiences and brings to light the clash of cultures which can cause misunderstandings between missionaries and Kenyans. The cross-cultural lessons learned in this book can be applied to missions anywhere.

Recovery: A Return to the Self
ISBN: 978-1-935434-51-1

Using real-life situations, the author demonstrates principles and practices to recover the true self lost along the way. The blueprint the author used in her own recovery is like a roadmap to protect and guide - not just a rule book. As a hospice chaplain, the author witnessed first-hand the wisdom of the dying, but it was after working with the poor and dying in India that she created the spiritual 12-step program outlined in this book.

Thinking Outside the Box ...About Love
ISBN: 978-1-935434-00-5

It begins with seeking and ends with discovery; it is a deeply personal story of warm hopes and cold realities. It is a journey of conviction, compelling both the writer and the reader to look at the world differently and start, Thinking Outside the Box.. About Love. This book tells of Donna in the role of VA Chaplain who demonstrates true, Christian love for the lost and suffering.

First Day Devotions

ISBN 978-1-935434-87-0

In my work as a Chaplain/Pastoral Care Coordinator at the Lexington Rescue Mission in Lexington, Kentucky, part of my job is to write a weekly devotional for the staff. Each Wednesday afternoon I sit in my office, pray, and write my devotion, then email it to all of the staff. Each week several of the Mission staff sends me wonderfully kind and uplifting feedback from my devotions, which I do not deserve, but give glory to God if the devotionals have touched hearts and minds. After doing this part of my job for a couple of months, I decided to compile these devotions into a small book that could be used not only for the staff, but also for clients, and perhaps in homes and churches. I have included many of the devotions written at the Mission in this book and pray God uses them to uplift you.

**These books may be ordered at
www.gea-books.com/bookstore or
from the Author at donnajunker@roadrunner.com
or any place good books are sold.**

Sources and References

- Chambers, Oswald. *My Utmost for His Highest.* "The Faith to Persevere." May 8, 2016, Discovery House Publishers: Grand Rapids, Michigan, 2016.

- Green, Hollis L. (translator) *The Evergreen Devotional New Testament* (EDNT). Complete Edition, Post-Gutenberg Books: Global Ed Advance Press, Nashville. 2015.

- Global Missions Health Conference, Southeast Christian Church, Louisville, KY. 2015.

- Hoffer, Eric. *The Passionate State of Mind: and Other Aphorisms.* Harper & Row Publishers: New York, New York, 1955.

- King, Dr. Martin Luther, "I Have a Dream." Speech given at the Lincoln Memorial in Washington D.C. on August 28, 1963.

- Luther, Dr. Martin. *Luther's Large Catechism*, April, 1529.

- Merton, Thomas: *Spiritual Master. The Essential Writings.* Edited by Lawrence S. Cunningham, Paulist Press, Mahwah, New Jersey: 1992.

- Metzger, Bruce M. and Murphy, Roland E. Editors, *The New Oxford Annotated Bible New Revised Version*, New York: Oxford University Press, 1994.

- Scalise, Eric, Ph.D. American Association of Christian Counselors, "Living and Serving in a Broken World: The Power of Relationship", Crisis Pregnancy Coaching 101, Light University: Forest, VA.

- Spafford, Horatio, "It Is Well With My Soul." Lyrics written by Horatio Spafford, music written by P. P, Bliss with Dwight L. Moody, 1873.

2018 Calendar

January 2018

Su	Mo	Tu	We	Th	Fr	Sa
	1	2	3	4	5	6
7	8	9	10	11	12	13
14	15	16	17	18	19	20
21	22	23	24	25	26	27
28	29	30	31			

February 2018

Su	Mo	Tu	We	Th	Fr	Sa
				1	2	3
4	5	6	7	8	9	10
11	12	13	14	15	16	17
18	19	20	21	22	23	24
25	26	27	28			

March 2018

Su	Mo	Tu	We	Th	Fr	Sa
				1	2	3
4	5	6	7	8	9	10
11	12	13	14	15	16	17
18	19	20	21	22	23	24
25	26	27	28	29	30	31

April 2018

Su	Mo	Tu	We	Th	Fr	Sa
1	2	3	4	5	6	7
8	9	10	11	12	13	14
15	16	17	18	19	20	21
22	23	24	25	26	27	28
29	30					

May 2018

Su	Mo	Tu	We	Th	Fr	Sa
		1	2	3	4	5
6	7	8	9	10	11	12
13	14	15	16	17	18	19
20	21	22	23	24	25	26
27	28	29	30	31		

June 2018

Su	Mo	Tu	We	Th	Fr	Sa
					1	2
3	4	5	6	7	8	9
10	11	12	13	14	15	16
17	18	19	20	21	22	23
24	25	26	27	28	29	30

July 2018

Su	Mo	Tu	We	Th	Fr	Sa
1	2	3	4	5	6	7
8	9	10	11	12	13	14
15	16	17	18	19	20	21
22	23	24	25	26	27	28
29	30	31				

August 2018

Su	Mo	Tu	We	Th	Fr	Sa
			1	2	3	4
5	6	7	8	9	10	11
12	13	14	15	16	17	18
19	20	21	22	23	24	25
26	27	28	29	30	31	

September 2018

Su	Mo	Tu	We	Th	Fr	Sa
						1
2	3	4	5	6	7	8
9	10	11	12	13	14	15
16	17	18	19	20	21	22
23	24	25	26	27	28	29
30						

October 2018

Su	Mo	Tu	We	Th	Fr	Sa
	1	2	3	4	5	6
7	8	9	10	11	12	13
14	15	16	17	18	19	20
21	22	23	24	25	26	27
28	29	30	31			

November 2018

Su	Mo	Tu	We	Th	Fr	Sa
				1	2	3
4	5	6	7	8	9	10
11	12	13	14	15	16	17
18	19	20	21	22	23	24
25	26	27	28	29	30	

December 2018

Su	Mo	Tu	We	Th	Fr	Sa
						1
2	3	4	5	6	7	8
9	10	11	12	13	14	15
16	17	18	19	20	21	22
23	24	25	26	27	28	29
30	31					

www.RocketCalendar.com

www.ingramcontent.com/pod-product-compliance
Lightning Source LLC
Chambersburg PA
CBHW021054090426
42738CB00006B/339